Classic ARNIS
The Legacy of Placido Yambao

D1519006

Reynaldo S. Galang

Classic **ARNIS**

DISCLAIMER

Please note that neither the author nor the publisher of this book is to be held responsible in any manner whatsoever for any injury that may result from practicing and/or following the techniques described within. The physical activities described herein may be too strenuous in nature for some readers to engage in safely. It is recommended that a physician be consulted prior to training.

Copyright 1992, 2004 by Reynaldo S. Galang

All rights reserved. No part of this book may be reproduced in any form or by any electronic or mechanical means, including information storage and retrieval systems, without permission in writing from the publisher, except by a reviewer who may use photos or quote brief passages in a review.

ISBN 0-9727679-0-8

Library of Congress Catalog Number: 2003117081

Published by:
arjee enterprises inc.
P. O. Box 692
Roseland, NJ 07068

Printed by:
Bookmasters, Inc.
Mansfield, Ohio

Dedicated to my uncle, "Daddy Pulis",
my first sponsor and mentor in the martial arts.

P/Major Jesus A. Songco (Ret.)
Western Police District - Metropolitan Police Force
Metro-Manila, Philippines

Classic **ARNIS**

Contents

Contents

The original cover of Placido Yambao's
Mga Karunungan sa Larong Arnis

Classic **ARNIS**

FOREWORD
by Christopher N. Ricketts

The book "Mga Karunungan sa Larong Arnis" is probably the oldest written manual on arnis published in the Philippines. Authored by Placido Yambao and written in Tagalog, it has long been out of print and is only available in the archives of the National Library of the Philippines.

It has been a much read book by researchers and scholars seeking to find resources into the indigenous martial arts of the Philippines. The late Edgar Sulite, Punong Guro of Lameco Eskrima International, came across this book while doing research for his book "The Secrets of Arnis". By chance, my good friend Alex Co was able to obtain this rare manuscript from a book collector. It was almost next to impossible to find this book outside of the library archives. Alex Co generously shared this find with me, Edgar Sulite and Rey Galang. Thus this project came into being.

Placido Yambao and Rey Galang share the common heritage of Pampanga's esoteric fighting art of Sinawali. Rey, using his knowledge in the languages and the arts, was more than capable to embark on the translation and re-illustration of the techniques presented in the original book. With his characteristic flair for structure and analysis, Rey Galang unravels, unveils and generously makes gift of the hidden treasures of Placido Yambao's legacy.

I'm glad that Rey Galang has undertaken the enormous task of making this historical book available in English and making this great contribution to the martial arts world. My congratulations to him for his continued preservation and propagation of the Warrior Arts of the Philippines.

Christopher N. Ricketts
Bakbakan International HQ
Metro-Manila, Philippines

FOREWORD
by Mark V. Wiley

It is an honor and gives me great pleasure to write the foreword to Reynaldo S. Galang's tribute to the legacy of Placido Yambao's rare and insightful book, *(Mga Karunungan Sa Larong Arnis) Knowledge in the Art of Arnis,* originally published in 1957. The importance of this book to the world of arnis cannot be overstated. Indeed, it is the first written record that we know of on the Filipino martial arts proper.

It is perhaps due to Yambao's archaic and purist use of the Tagalog language that kept it from becoming popular and a ready source of techniques among the *arnisadores* of its time. Indeed, even today, many native Tagalog speakers are unable to effectively read (let alone translate) the original. And while there are only a few original copies of the book in existence, many have tried to recreate Yambao's art from third and fourth generation photocopies of the original text. Many more have copied and perpetuated its historical presentation of the art without caring if it was correct or not. Indeed, much of the history of the art presented has been proven inaccurate through the anthropological record.

Aside from being a novelty or collector's item, the greatest value of this book is found in the presentation of the physical characteristics of the art of *espada y daga* as practiced in the first half of the 20th century – an art that is so rarely seen today, even in the Philippines. This book is a gem of discovery as it holds many of the obscure but effective fighting techniques of *espada y daga*, the classical Filipino art of sword and dagger fighting. Indeed, this book is an ethnograph of the Filipino art of weaponry during a time and place when armed challenge matches between arnisadores was commonplace. It is a moment of discovery and analysis of arnis based on the knowledge and experience of its contributors: Placido Yambao, Buenaventura Mirafuente, Luis Cruz, Juan Aclan, and Francisco de la Cruz – all well-established and proven combatants.

This book is also important on a sociological level, as it records the place of arnis in the minds of the non-practicing Filipino. Editor Buenaventura Mirafuente begins his *"Short History of Arnis"* with the simple phrase: *"Arnis should become a national sport."* The word *"should"* is an indication that, even in the 1950s, and like today, the art of arnis was not widely embraced by Filipinos.

Even with the original publication of this book, the authors were unsuccessful in making arnis a national sport. And although Remy Presas later successfully introduced a "modern" version of arnis into the public education system during the 1970s, the art of arnis still eluded most Filipinos, who consider *"things Filipino"* to be of lesser quality and importance than *"things foreign."* Such a

10

mentality is seen in the languages, clothing styles, and musical preferences of Filipinos today, and is a reflection of the colonial mentality forced on them by Spanish and American colonizers. Perhaps most disturbing is that while arnis has been in existence for generations and is that which helped the Filipinos to fight and fend off foreign invaders, there are talks of taekwondo becoming the national sport of the Philippines!

I salute Master Reynaldo S. Galang, the author of this book, without whom Placido Yambao's legacy would undoubtedly remain an enigma. This book is not only a translation by Master Rey, but includes his commentaries and supplementary materials on the art. It is through his commentaries and insights that the classical art of espada y daga, as practiced in the 1950s, can finally be examined properly. Perhaps by bringing the book back in print, it will show the Filipinos that their indigenous martial arts are not only loved by many and practiced around the world, but important enough for this individual to have a book they cared nothing about translated into English and brought into world martial arts consciousness. With this, it is hoped that the art of arnis will continue to evolve, spread, and exist in the coming millenium – to one day become the national sport of the Philippines and embraced by Filipinos worldwide.

Mark V. Wiley
Author: Filipino Martial Culture
         Filipino Fighting Arts
         Cabales Serrada Eskrima

FOREWORD
by Kelly S. Worden

Forged in the fire of life, the science and art of Classic Arnis "Mga Karunungan sa Larong Arnis", written by Placido Yambao and finally made available in English by Reynaldo S. Galang, will surely impact generations of arnisadors in years to come.

As a practitioner of Modern Arnis, I am humbled by the request to provide a written foreword to this treasured and valued resource. This historical treatise and translation is both a new beginning and a record of days gone by.

The practical knowledge and presentation of the art is important, not just for beauty or embellishment, but for the balance of efficiency in combat. The resurgence of this historical Filipino literary work is a tribute to the unprecedented level of interest and worldwide acceptance of arnis as a combat form today. Contained within is an anthology of concepts, unique and effective, capturing the very essence of the Filipino warrior spirit.

Without question, the written contributions in this book by such great fighters and educators in arnis history such as Buenaventura Mirafuente, Luis Cruz, Francisco de la Cruz and Juan Aclan blend passion and lore with the rudiments of classic arnis, literally the stuff of legend.

Unconquerable spirit is an essential part of the education and discipline derived from the practice of arnis. Modern practitioners have the opportunity to feel the connection of historical insights into an art that has struggled to survive and has now gained respect and prominence in the fighting arts worldwide.

Although I am personally intrigued by the historical significance of Placido Yambao's research and documentation, I feel the true value and diversity of arnis is yet to be realized. It is my belief that through the unselfish efforts of individuals such as Rey Galang, the physical fighting structure, heritage and evolution of Filipino Martial Arts will continue to be developed, refined and preserved.

Currently here in the United States, U. S. military, law enforcement, and serious civilians have realized the prominence of arnis as a highly effective method of self defense. Countless programs have been introduced not only to develop technical proficiency but also for the benefit of refining both physiological and psychological attributes during conflicts and gain important insight into the reality of close quarter combat.

We, the current generation of arnis practitioners and instructors, owe a debt of gratitude to those warriors of the art that forged the path for us to discover the functional beauty of arnis.

Wisdom, discipline, and defense are the key spiritual connections we all share with those who came first. Honor their commitment and treasure the dedication to their Filipino cultural roots.

Humbly within the Art,

Kelly S. Worden
Student, friend and brother in life of my mentor, Grandmaster Remy A. Presas.

FOREWORD
by Conrado N. Rigor Jr.

The Filipinos are a happy mixture of several races --- Malay, basically, with Chinese, Indian, Spanish and American blends. The result is what makes that formula uniquely Filipino. And that goes as well with all other skills Filipinos come up with.

Concededly, Filipinos are now the most exported Asians in the free world. They are almost in every country on the planet. Their expertise and skills run the length and breadth of every human endeavor --- from the humble pipe-layer in the Middle East, to the hardy woodcutter in the frigid forests of Eastern Europe, to the creative animators of flighty American films, to breaking notoriously into heretofore high-tech and secured computer systems, to the sophisticated research laboratories of the space exploration program --- Filipinos are finding their niches and carving their marks.

One distinct area that the Filipino has made exceptional contribution to is in the pre-eminent field of martial arts. Known only to discriminating practitioners, the Filipino martial artist has developed his skills through the merging of Oriental and Western techniques and training. The results are highly distinctive combat forms that discerning military units of industrialized nations have come to embrace. The sensible, efficient and smooth executions, paramount to life-and-death situations, are held in high regard. This is one reason why, in hand-to-hand or infighting guerilla warfare and survival, the Filipino's expertise is widely (and often secretly) sought.

Historians affirm that before the advent of the Spaniards, proud warriors of the Philippine archipelago had long practiced their own form of combat arts. Such fighting techniques had been handed down through the ages and have been refined with every generation's eminent Guro (teacher).

For more than three decades, Guro and author Rey Galang, a dedicated disciple of the enduring warrior arts of his forefathers, has remained steadfast to the strict and demanding code of the Filipino martial arts. He is regarded today as one of the Philippines' foremost practitioners of deadly bladed weaponry. Although Rey had years of martial arts training in the oriental disciplines of judo, jiu-jitsu, karate, arnis and taekwondo, his specialty has been refined by extensive studies of the fabled blade-wielding artists of past generations in Central Luzon. He had learned and practiced the art under legendary mentors and then refined his own techniques with his peer group in Bakbakan International, a worldwide outfit that he had helped form with other equally dedicated and respected Filipino martial artists.

14

This widely-researched book is another of Rey's projects to consolidate his passion for the Warrior Arts of the Philippines. His aim: for future generations to gain priceless perspective into an enduring Filipino warrior art. Most of it is now part and parcel of the arsenal of combat skills that specialized military organizations hold with pride and confidence. Today, soldiers trained by Rey's group are fielded in critical regions of conflict in the name of liberty and freedom. Indeed, the painstaking, intricate but deeply respected warrior art espoused by Rey Galang and his zealous band is one more testament to the Filipino's broad contribution towards maintaining harmony and balance in a competitive, helter-skelter world.

Conrado "Sluggo" N. Rigor Jr.
Publisher and Editor
Filipino-American Bulletin
Seattle, WA

FOREWORD
(from the original edition)
by Luis Cruz

To the Reader:

This book, written by Placido Yambao and edited by Buenaventura Mirafuente, is truly exceptional and could be compared with the best of our existing literary works. This is not a book of fantasy or of imagination. It is neither a treatise on philosophy or the sciences, nor is it a book of poetry or dreams. It summarizes the result of extensive research, incomparable experience and dedication to the combat art of arnis.

This publication is the culmination of the author's many years of practicing, performing, teaching and competing in the art of arnis. From competitions held at the Olympic Stadium (since 1927) to the countless provincial and town tournaments, Placido Yambao has managed to distill into this single unique book his experience and knowledge in the art of arnis.

You will learn the rudiments of the "alpabeto", i.e., the names of the strikes. The "abakada" or basic drills will teach you the different forms, up to and including the 10 regla (forms) that comprise all the strikes and blocks. In general, this book will give you a deeper understanding and appreciation of the art of arnis.

After the exposition of the 10 regla or forms, which are demonstrated in this book using strikes and blocks, the eight set of drills which follow give the different striking techniques and combinations useful in gaining advantage over one's opponent. In the study of this book, you will discover how the art of arnis will contribute to your physical well being. These benefits are primarily in the areas of health, strength, exercise and the development of skill in the art of self-defense.

Prior to the end of this book, you will find the following three major topics:

a. Rules and Regulations
   - Rules of arnis
   - Duties and Responsibilities of the Referee
   - Duties and Responsibilities of the Judges

b. Arnis Protocol
   The meaning of weapon salutations in Arnis.

c. Arnis Drills and Exercises
   The use of arnis as a physical exercise program for inclusion in the regular school curriculum.

I ask the reader to hold this book in high esteem and to patronize the art of arnis both in mind and spirit, and to always remember that the art of arnis is indigenous to the Philippines. This art has been the sole shield and weapon of our heroes and warriors in the Revolution of 1896. It sustained them onward through countless battles in the fight for freedom and in defense of their beloved motherland until the flag of the lost republic of Malolos once again waved proudly and heralded the voice of freedom.

I also beseech our government and all those concerned to support the art of Arnis as a national sport and to seek the inclusion of arnis in our schools throughout this brave land of ours.

Luis Cruz
Hagonoy, Bulacan

The sections on Arnis Protocol and Duties and Responsiblities of the Referee and Judges are not included in this book for the following reasons:

Organizational and regional methods of proper arnis etiquette and protocol are so varied that a clearly and explicitly spoken agreement is a far better (and safer) method of communicating the intent and scope of the encounter.

Likewise, the rules and regulations concerning arnis competition and the conduct thereof are based on existing practice at the time the original manuscript was written. Similarities may exist with current practice but not necessarily be the same. These vary from region to region and between organizations.

The drills and exercises, which basically was a recap of the abakadas, are replaced by the original exercises and drills from the art of Sinawali. In addition, the the double stick form "Dimasupil" is included to give the reader a more profound insight into the mother art of Placido Yambao and his colleagues. The drills represent a detailed breakdown of the components and techniques found in "Dimasupil".

INTRODUCTION
by Reynaldo S. Galang

For nearly half a century, the work of Placido Yambao has interested and intrigued Filipino Martial Arts (FMA) aficionados all over the world. Yambao's book was the first widely released documentation of a popular and, at the same time, obscure art. The book was the primary reference used by many FMA authors for details on the history of arnis.

Placido Yambao and his colleagues, in their own way, were able to pre-serve the priceless legacy of the Warrior Arts of the Philippines. Despite the haphazard illustrations and notations used in the original book as well as the classic and archaic language and phraseology, the manuscript managed to safe-guard the art's many overt and hidden treasures. Taking advantage of the scarcity of this book, unscrupulous writers have blatantly ransacked Placido Yambao's work while making specious claims of ownership and originality.

With the publication of this book, we hope to clarify and credit the true origin and seed of this plundered knowledge. The reader will discover familiar terms whose origin and exclusive ownership have been ambiguously claimed by other FMA systems. Yambao and his colleagues were unselfishly focused on documenting the art, as it was practiced in their days, and in sharing it with the general public. They liberally shared this generous legacy with the Filipino people and the martial arts world.

Those who used Yambao's work as the basis of their "system" barely scratched the surface and only managed to present it from the single weapon perspective. This despite the fact that the entire work focused on two-weapon combinations using sword and dagger techniques. One can only surmise that this banality was the result of lack of understanding and inadequate knowledge of Yambao's art.

Placido Yambao hails from the province of Pampanga, a province known for its many fierce warriors and leaders. It also is the source of the art of "Adwang Mutun" (two sticks) or Sinawali (sinauali). Prior to its becoming popular under the name arnis, the art, in general, was popularly and cross-regionally known as kali - taken from the word kalis (meaning sword) from the Capampangan (Amanung Sisuan) language (or dialect, depending on the reader's perspective). The word kalis is not exclusively Capampangan and appears in many other regional dialects, always bearing the same meaning. This is further explained in Buenaventura Mirafuente's article and footnotes on the history of arnis, the entire text of which is included in this book.

Pampanga historians write of the martial training of Pampango men garbed in white, moving swiftly and smoothly like ghosts under the pale moonlight. They trained with their "mutuns" rubbed with soot, making the "vanquished" easily identifiable. From this province come some of the notable practitioners and leaders of the art. The famous brothers Placido and Pedro Puno (Sirung and Iru) as well as Pablo Bautista (Apung Ambu) hail from Macabebe. Maestro Bonifacio comes from Masantol, Maestro Navarro from Paralaya and the renowned Alfonso Gagui Clarin (Tatang Osung) from Pulung Butul, Santa Cruz. From Tarlac comes Anastacio Alimurung (Maestro Tasyu) as well as Aurelio Sangalang (Maestro Eliung), and from Apalit, Maestro Joaquin Galang. The noted Tatang Osung Clarin was known as the Lakantalaturu (chief instructor) of the style known as "Cuentada". The controversial and fierce Macabebe mercenaries also come from this province.

Sinawali or Adwang Mutun was the root of the system and techniques that Yambao's manuscript preserved and shared with the general public. The repetitive use of the same photos to demonstrate different phases of the action tended to confuse the reader and student since the sequence of the photos showed the participants inexplicably changing positions as well as photo locations. One can only speculate whether Yambao intentionally tried to conceal the gems of the art or the austere use of available photos was a question of economics. He did, however, leave a wealth of treasure behind to be found by those who commenced with the knowledge and skill of his mother art and diligently followed the path laid out.

In effect, Yambao's book is like a mysterious and beckoning treasure map, to be understood, followed and completed successfully by those who took the pain and trouble of equipping themselves with the same knowledge and skill as that of the original explorers. Without this perspective, one can easily and totally get lost and confused trying to imitate without understanding. Without this knowledge, erroneous assumptions can be made in trying to bridge the gaps without the span of details that Yambao takes for granted.

The original book, generally and erroneously assumed to be a primer to the art, actually serves as a reference or advanced reading for the well-versed practitioner. In many aspects, Yambao's text assumes that the reader is already knowledgeable and thus sparingly explains and describes the rudiments and combinations of the techniques, making it a bewildering and challenging resource even to the initiated.

This book was initially intended as a straightforward contextual translation. However, it soon became apparent that Yambao's classic art of arnis could be given new life by reorganizing and expanding the material and presenting it in a way that benefits both beginning and advanced practitioners of the art.

With this book, we share with you Yambao's priceless and timeless legacy. With this book we share with the reader the heritage of the Warrior Arts of the Philippines.

Reynaldo S. Galang
Chief Instructor
Bakbakan International (WHQ)
Lodi, New Jersey

INTRODUCTION

(from the original edition)
by Placido Yambao

The art of weaponry and the different techniques of strikes, thrusts and blocks within each and every drill (abakada) is demonstrated and described in detail in this book. The techniques and demonstrations are performed by the author, Placido Yambao, the editor, Buenaventura Mirafuente and two noted teachers of the art, namely, Luis Cruz and Juan Aclan. It is the author's desire that this book give the reader a thorough understanding and knowledge of the art of arnis. Anyone who desires to have knowledge, understanding and skills in the art of arnis should seriously study and follow this book and adopt the techniques and drills demonstrated.

My fellow countrymen and readers, this book has been written to impart my limited knowledge of the art of arnis with the sole intention of sharing our native art with you. It is my fervent hope that our indigenous art of arnis will serve and assist our youth in developing into the leaders of tomorrow. Never forget that arnis is our primary martial art and is not just a sport. It has been a weapon and a shield to our past heroes beginning with Lapulapu in 1521 to the Revolution of 1896.

This book also intends to reveal to the rest of the world that we Filipinos have our native sports, specifically arnis. It is our very own combat art, which should be used to develop physical strength and superior skills in martial arts.

I ask you, fellow readers, to forgive any inadequacies that my writing skills may have. Please accept my feeble attempt at writing as a simple desire to propagate and perpetuate the art of arnis.

Placido Yambao
Hagonoy, Bulacan

ACKNOWLEDGEMENT

This project would never have seen the light of day if not for the selfless contribution and support made by many people.

- Alex Co and Ramon Villardo who generously shared their rare and precious original copies of Placido Yambao's book with me.

- Christopher Ricketts, Tony Diego, and the late Edgar Sulite, true and dedicated martial artists, who shared the excitement and rewards of finding this treasured legacy.

- Mark V. Wiley and Alexander D. Kask who, having seen my first contextual translation of the book, encouraged me to pursue this project.

- Ramon Martinez of the Classical and Historical Fencing Association who saw and recognized the fraternity of the blade reaching across culture and time.

- Kelly Worden and Conrado Rigor who supported us in our American northwest activities.

- My wife, Marilen Friedlander Galang, for typing and proofreading the manuscript; Carlos Aldrete, for meticulously scanning the original images; and Richard N. Sullivan, for final proofreading.

- All members and students of Bakbakan International specially those who participated in this project.

Steve Antonsson	Carl Figueroa
Wileen Arellano	John Jacobo
Michael Beach	Rob Jacobo
Chris Bengel	Wilson Lopez
Alex Bird	Rich Riccardi
Dexter Brown	Alain Salvo
Xavier Chavez	Ken Sato
Carlos Cobles	Ray Tibayan
Jose Cobles	Jim Young
Alex Delanuez	

Sa inyong lahat, maraming salamat....

Reynaldo S. Galang
Chief Instructor
Bakbakan International (WHQ)
Lodi, New Jersey

PROFILE

PLACIDO YAMBAO

The author of "Mga Karunungan Sa Larong Arnis" is a well-known instructor in the art of Arnis and one of the organizers of "Kapisanang Dunong at Lakas, (Tabak Ni Bonifacio, 1946)" (*translation: Association of Knowledge and Strength, The Sword of Bonifacio, 1946*). The aforementioned organization was comprised of enthusiasts in the art of arnis of which Yambao was president for five years (1934-38). The author started practicing the art of arnis in 1925 and is regarded as one of the art's premier exponents. He has competed several times at the Olympic Stadium and in numerous provincial tournaments.

Yambao was awarded a Teaching Diploma (Guro) in the art of arnis by the Magtanggol [Defender] Sporting Club under the auspices of Joaquin Galang. He became the chief instructor of this club and was a devoted champion of any undertaking that advanced and promoted the art of Arnis.

Placido Yambao performed and introduced the different types of blocks in the 5th to the 8th Abakada. He also performed and demonstrated the different strikes from the 1st to the 4th Abakada.

PROFILE

BUENAVENTURA MIRAFUENTE

Buenaventura Mirafuente organized and edited the book "Mga Karunungan Sa Larong Arnis" to conform with what was then the current practice of arnis. He began his study of arnis in 1931 and was President of the Instructor's Committee for the Kapisanang Dunong at Lakas (1931-38). Mirafuente is a dedicated participant at all demonstrations, competitions and promotions in the art of arnis. He was president of the Kapisanang Dunong at Lakas from 1938-1943 and president of Tabak ni Bonifacio from 1949 up to the writing of this book (1957).

Mirafuente organized the resolution presented to the Municipal Council of Manila on the 29th of April, 1954, with the help of Tundo Councilor Dr. Marciano Santos and other supporters. This organization proposed that the art of arnis be taught in the High Schools of the City of Manila. This was ratified on the 6th of August, 1954.

Buenaventura Mirafuente demonstrated the striking techniques from the 5th to the 8th Abakada with Placido Yambao performing the blocks.

PROFILE

LUIS CRUZ

Luis Cruz is a teacher and an expert in the art of arnis. He is noted for his extensive experience in teaching, demonstrating and competing in arnis in various towns, provinces, organizations and schools since 1936. Cruz was secretary of the Kapisanang Dunong at Lakas and of the Tabak Ni Bonifacio organizations.

Luis Cruz performed and demonstrated the blocks in the 1st to the 4th Abakada with Placido Yambao.

PROFILE

JUAN ACLAN

Juan Aclan is one of the most distinguished and best exponents of arnis from the province of Batangas. He has participated in several competitions in different towns and provinces. Aclan is a dedicated supporter and participant in all activities and competitions in the art of arnis all over Luzon. He was the secretary of the Kapisanang Dunong at Lakas from 1929 to 1948.

Luis Aclan performed the blocks in the 9th to the 10th Abakada with Luis Cruz.

PROFILE

FRANCISCO DE LA CRUZ

Francisco de la Cruz started the study of arnis in 1920. He has participated in numerous competitions in several towns and provinces, De la Cruz organized the Kapisanang Dunong at Lakas on the 26th of August, 1927. This association was composed of devotees and supporters of the art of arnis.

Francisco de la Cruz is an accredited instructor and holds a wealth of experience in the teaching and promotion of the art of arnis.

Franciso de la Cruz does not appear as a direct participant but was instrumental in the actual compilation and publication of the manuscript.

PROFILE

REYNALDO S. GALANG

Reynaldo S. Galang is co-founder of Bakbakan International and is the organization's International Director. He is one of the designated Senior Instructors of the art of Kali Ilustrisimo by Grand Master Antonio Ilustrisimo. Galang is also one of the premier organizers and developers of the art of Bakbakan Kali which is a highly structured and expanded version of Kali Ilustrisimo.

Rey Galang is internationally known for his dedication to the support, development and promotion of the warrior arts of the Philippines. Galang is also the recognized and appointed Chief Instructor of the arts of Tulisan, Hagibis, and Sinawali. He has trained and produced countless champions in the Filipino Martial Arts. Galang conducts classes on the Philippine combat arts at the Bakbakan organization's World Headquarters (WHQ) in Lodi, New Jersey, USA.

A Brief History of Arnis

(from the original edition)
by Buenaventura Mirafuente

<u>Arnis should become a national sport.</u>

There is no reason why arnis, our heritage's art of self-defense, should not become the national sport of the Philippines. It should hold a national status similar to the sport of baseball in the United States, rugby in England, kendo and sumo in Japan, bullfighting in Spain, and others.

Dr. Jose Rizal, Gen. Antonio Luna, Gen. Gregorio del Pilar, Gat Andres Bonifacio, Rev. Father Gregorio Aglipay and other heroes of our race were all experts in the art of arnis. Aside from the known virtues of this art (i.e., as a combative and self-defense art), it also promotes strength and physical well being.

Arnis develops the upper body and strengthens the lungs. Anyone who practices arnis automatically trims off fat from his body, reduces nervousness and stress, and eliminates dyspepsia. Arnis is a sight to behold, whether as a sport or actual combat. Anyone who practices the art of arnis develops keen eyes, anticipates the movements and intentions of the opponent, improves the strategic positioning and handling of his weapon, and develops his timing. The overall result is a strong defense and weapon in combat and self-defense.

<u>Arnis amazes Legazpi.</u>

In 1564, 43 years after the discovery of the Philippine Islands by Don Fernando Magellan, Don Miguel Lopez de Legazpi and his 380 armed Spanish soldiers found the natives skillful in the art of arnis, an art similar to the sword and dagger techniques of Europe.

When Legazpi arrived in Abuyog, Leyte, in the middle of February 1564, he and his soldiers were overjoyed with the reception given them by Chief Malitik of Leyte and his son, Kamutuhan. The festivity was in honor of their esteemed royal guests who greatly enjoyed the native dances, wrestling and the display of arnis, which at that time was commonly called kali[1]. The martial art demonstration was the highlight of the occasion.

After the celebration, Kamutuhan accompanied Legazpi to Limasawa where once again a warm reception was given to the guests and more demonstrations of kali were presented. When Legazpi arrived in Kamiging on March 1564, the festivities in their honor once again included the demonstration of the combat art of kali. Chief Sikatuna of Bohol warmly received Legazpi and a blood compact sealed the friendship between the two illustrious leaders. During the celebration commemorating the memorable event, an exhibition of arnis dominated the festivities. Chief Pambuwaya of Dapitan also gave a similar reception for Legazpi. On April 27, 1564, Legazpi arrived in Cebu and met Chief Tupas and his renowned, fierce warriors. Legazpi witnessed the excellent warrior skills of Chief Tupas' soldiers in the art of

kali. Legazpi commented that "kali is not only a pleasant sport and enchanting art but a very effective combat art for the battlefields."

Legazpi was totally amazed at the unexpected degree of the natives' martial skills.

Recalling the tragic end suffered by Magellan in the hands of similar native warriors, Legazpi took extra steps to cultivate his friendship with Chief Tupas. Fortunately their friendship developed to the point that Chief Tupas was converted and baptized in the Christian faith on June 1, 1564. Chief Tupas was christened Don Felipe in honor of King Philip of Spain.

Due to the rarity and lack of adequate historical details regarding the origin of the art of arnis (kali), this writer assumes that the art was brought over by the Malay people (from *taga-malayo* - people from afar) when they arrived in the Philippines.

Arnis was known as kali up to 1610.

In the early days, our ancestors knew the art of arnis as kali. However, as time passes, changes are unavoidable and it became known as "Pananandata" in Tagalog, "Pagkalikali" in the plains of Cagayan by the Ibanags, "Kalirongan" in Pangasinan, "Kaliradman" in Visaya and "Pagaradman" in Ilongo in 1860, "Didya" in Ilocos and, in 1872, came to be called "Kabaroan". This is according to Rev. Fr. Gregorio Aglipay, a noted arnis practitioner[2].

After the Philippines had been colonized for a period of over a hundred years, the recreational forms of "moro-moro" and "duplo" came to the attention of the Spanish clergy. These forms of entertainment concealed the martial application of Arnis and therefore, enabled the practice of the art to continue. The word arnis was derived from the Spanish word "arnes" used to describe the colorful trimmings used by the performers of moro-moro and duplo. These trimmings identified the rank and role of each character as well as overt affiliation, either as a Christian or an infidel.

In 1853 the name kali was replaced by arnis after the noted writer/orator Balagtas wrote about arnis in his epic *Florante at Laura* wherein he describes the demonstration of knowledge and skill in the arts of wrestling (buno) and arnis as part of the festivities.

"Minulan ang galit sa pagsasayawan
ayon sa musika't awit na saliwan,
larong buno't arnes na kinakitaan
ng kanikaniyang liksi't karunungan."

A Brief History of Arnis

Dancing infused with burning intensity
driven by a song and music of fury
displays of wrestling and arnis enjoyed
brilliant skills and tactics employed.

Why were the Filipinos excellent in arnis during this period?

Guns were neither common nor easily available to Filipinos in those days. It was therefore practical to develop and continue to use for defense and combat whatever weapons were available. The premier experts in the art of arnis were the nobility and warlords of the Visayan and Tagalog regions, for example Amandakwa in Pangasinan and Baruwang from the plains of Cagayan. It is for this reason that arnis was known to be "the Art of the Kings." The prominent warriors of those days were well known for their skill in the use of the tabak, kampilan, dagger, spear and for their prowess in archery.

Arnis demonstrations and competitions were a major form of entertainment during fiestas, weddings, christenings, cockfights and special holidays or celebrations in honor of the tribal gods, or the noble leaders and guests. In times of war, the authorities launched major efforts to teach military and weaponry skills to their citizenry. For close quarters combat skills development, the citizens were trained in the use of mid-range and close quarter weapons, namely, espada y daga techniques. These very same skills were also used to settle feuds and misunderstandings.

Due to these developments, arnis became an integral part of Filipino life. As a result, secret training centers and associations blossomed under the protection of the Filipino freedom fighters. The underground leaders, our heroes-to-be, recognized the need for a prepared and well-trained group of people to lead in the fight for freedom against the colonists who had oppressed and subjugated the Philippines since 1521.

Several years before the revolution of 1896, Don Jose de Azas opened the Tanghalan ng Sandata (Hall of Arms) on Sales Street in Manila. This school openly taught the arts of weaponry, and in Ateneo de Manila, arnis and fencing were taught exclusive of the academic subjects. It was here that many of our heroes learned the art of European fencing in addition to the native art of arnis.

Arnis is introduced to the world.

A historic proof of the Filipino's long existing expertise in arnis is cited in the record of the events of April 27, 1521. It was on this Saturday that Don Ferdinand Magellan and his Spanish army attacked the island of Mactan that was defended by Lapulapu and his warriors. It was an encounter that the Spaniards would never forget. Lapulapu and his warriors, armed with native swords, daggers

A Brief History of Arnis

and fire-hardened wooden spears, fought fiercely and bravely and defeated the well-equipped Spanish solders. As history shows, Magellan met his death in this bloody encounter. Spanish history records (Pigafetta) described the use of a great kampilan sword that resulted in the demise of the famed discoverer of the Philippines as:

> uno de ellos con gran terzado (kampilan) que equivale
> un gran cimitarra, le dio en la pierna izquierdan gran
> tajo que le hizo caeer de bruces... Esta funesta
> batallia se dio el 27 de Abril, 1521, Sabado.

> … one of the natives with a big sword (kampilan), the equivalent of a big scimitar delivered a powerful blow to his (Magellan) left leg causing him to fall... This battle took place on Saturday, the 27th day of April 1521.

The Spanish soldiers, seeing the fall of their leader, Magellan, hastily retreated to their ships to escape annihilation by the native "infidels."

When Legazpi, with Martin de Goiti, Juan de Salcedo, 120 soldiers and several Visayan guides, travelled to northern Luzon, they were fiercely resisted by the tribes of Rajah Lakan Dula and Rajah Soliman using cannons and bladed weapons made of cast iron by the famous Panday Pira of Pampanga.

It is a known fact that the primary weapons of the Filipinos in their fight against colonist oppression were the native sword and dagger. In the Revolution of 1896, the native sword, tabak, was the principal brandished weapon in the fight for freedom. The Japanese army, during World War II, faced the dreaded "Bolo Regiments" in jungle skirmishes.

All of our history is filled with tales of heroism and gallantry, and of heroes who used their skills in arnis to fight for their principles and freedom.

The art of arnis is suppressed.

From 1569, numerous Filipinos, in their desire to be recognized as enlightened Filipinos, embraced the Catholic faith and altogether abandoned the native arts and culture, including arnis. Kali, which was a popular pastime, was limited to being performed only during special occasions. In 1764, Don Simon de Anda y Salazar prohibited the performance of any sport. As a result, arnis almost disappeared from the Filipino culture except for those who lived far from the cities and towns and those who were not converts and were therefore immune from the pyschological hold of the priests.

A Brief History of Arnis

Because of the Filipinos' fanatic and obsessive attitude toward anything that they do and enjoy, the activities of moro-moro and duplo consumed most of their time resulting in the farms being neglected. As a consequence of this, the Spanish authorities prohibited the performance of any sport or leisure activity.

The priests had sole authority in selecting who may participate in regulated performances of moro-moro and duplo. Ironically, it was in the convents and monasteries that the art of arnis continued to flourish, its practice hidden within the theatrical guise of the moro-moro plays.

One of the primary reasons for the ban on the practice of arnis were the unavoidable deaths that resulted from the initial horse play between skilled arnis experts that inevitably escalated to actual life and death duels. In fiestas and other celebrations, it was common for arnis practitioners, under the influence of liquor as well as the cajoling of friends and hecklers, to engage in mortal combat to prove their skill and manhood. This led to the ban on the carrying of any bladed weapon, including the ubiquitious farm implement "itak" and the utilitarian "balaraw" or dagger.

Arnis should be taught in schools.

Antonio A. Maceda, Superintendent for City of Manila High Schools, made this statement to the author during a recent interview at his City Hall office: "If the game of cock fighting, a sport brought to this land by the Spanish "guachinangos", could become a national pastime, then more so should arnis and sipa (a native version of football) be encouraged to be developed nationally. These sports are not only indigenous to our country but they also produce physical well being and discipline in all. It is important that this art of self-defense be taught in our schools as part of our physical education program." The military and police applications of this art are of tremendous value as well. If we teach our native dances in schools, then all the more so should we teach arnis, an art that will strengthen our people and our defense forces.

It is known that in Europe and America, the art of fencing is encouraged and preserved, this being the identifiable form of defense attributed to their culture. We should likewise take steps to preserve and propagate the art of arnis by making it a national sport and teaching it to the leaders of tomorrow.

It is the belief of the author that it was Balagtas who first noticed the lack of support that Filipinos showed for local culture and art, including arnis. It is for this reason that he substituted the word "kalis" for sword, obviously referring to kali, in his immortal classic *Florante at Laura*. He used the might of his literary skills to preserve the art within his writings knowing that his works are read throughout the land.

A Brief History of Arnis

"Makita ng piling Heneral Osmalic
ang aking marahas na pamimiyapis,
pitong susong hanay ng dulo ng kalis
hinawi ng tabak nang ako'y masapit."

"Seeing my arrogant and brash attitude,
General Osmalic strove forward
With a single stroke swept away,
seven rows of brandished swords."

Buenaventura Mirafuente
President
Ang Tabak Ni Bonifacio, 1927
(Kapisanan ng Manlalaro ng Arnis sa Pilipinas)
Member: Philippine Library Association
       Biographical Society of the Philippines

Footnote:

1   Kali is the original name of the art of arnis prior to the arrival of the Spaniards in the Philippines. The kalis, from the word kali, is a sword of fine make and is used in kali. This was an ubiquitous side arm that men carried with them everywhere. If the letter "s" is added to the word kali, creating the word kalis, the meaning becomes a sword or machete, or a type of implement far longer than the ordinary tabak or agricultural implement that is in use today. "The maker of kalis is called an espader" says Tomas Pinpin in his book "Paaralan ng Wikang Kastila (A Study of the Spanish Language), published in Manila, 1610.

2   (a) Pananandata (Tagalog) 1. The art of the use of "kalis" (sword) and balaraw (dagger) in sports competition or mortal combat. 2. Proper knowledge of arms and weaponry that is used to conquer, win and kill victoriously in combat. 3. A contest that demonstrates and exemplifies the true and correct techniques and skills in the art of arms. 4. A tournament or competition that matches art against art and strength against strength in the use of weapons - tabak (kalis) and balaraw.

      (b) Pagkalikali (Ibanag - includes all the plains of Cagayan) - A contest or duel between armed participants. 2. A demonstration of skills and knowledge in the art of "armas de mano" - tabak and balaraw.

      (c) Kalirongan (Pangasinan) 1. A contest or duel that exemplifies the courage, special skills, expertise and strength of the participants. Should there be no clear winners in the art of armed combat, the participants continue without weapons and demonstrate their individual skills, speed, techniques and form.

      (d) Kaliradman (Visaya) 1. A duel of honor to resolve the cause of the conflict. 2. An honorable competion or duel. Pagaradman (Visaya - Ilonggo) 1. A fight to the death. 2. A sport or physical contest. 3. A physical regimen or exercise that demonstrates individual skills, speed, technques and form.

      (e) Didya (Ilocano) - Same as the Visayan interpretation. Kabaroan is an improved version of didya.

Notes on Teaching Arnis

(from the original edition)

Items of importance that should be understood in following this book.

1. The weapons used are called Tabak and Balaraw (Espada y Daga, Sword and Dagger).

Tabak is 32 inches in length and the Balaraw is 12 inches in length. The Tabak is held in the right hand and the Balaraw is held with the left hand.

2. If the instructor gives the command to thrust or block with the left weapon (kaliwa), then execute a thrust or a block with the balaraw. Accordingly do the same when instructed to thrust or strike with the right weapon (kanan).

3. If the instructor directs you to retract (urong) or step forward (sulong) with your foot then it is important that you should either take a step backward or a step forward. It will be made clear by the instructor as to which foot he is referring to. Everything will depend on the type of regla (form) or abakada (drill) being executed.

4. Because this book demonstrates the art and practice of arnis for sport and physical exercise, the tabak and balaraw mentioned and illustrated in this book are not real weapons but facsimiles for practice and training purposes only.

5. The first thing to be done at the commencement of instructions is to draw a straight line on which the practitioner is to place both feet. This will form the base from which all techniques are to be executed. When moving forward or backward, one foot must remain identified with this base position.

This set of instructions has been written to guide the reader and avoid confusion in the execution of any of the steps demonstrated in this book.

If there is any confusion or inconsistency in the presentations in this book, we beg the reader's indulgence and extend our apologies. Such errors are not intentional and are purely the results of this writer's (Yambao) inadequate writing abilities.

Placido Yambao

The Art of Weaponry

(from the original edition)

Arnis or Eskrima is divided into four (4) different types and art of weaponry as follows:

1. Muestracion - the exhibition or demonstration of individual skills thru striking and blocking.
2. Sangga at Patama - a demonstration of striking, blocking, and corresponding counter-attacks between two players.
3. Labanang Malapitan - close quarters combat
4. Labanang Malayuan - long range fighting

The above are known and recognized in the art of arnis by the following names:

- Muestracion
- Defensa ofensiva (sangga at patama)
- Rompido (close quarters combat)
- Larga Mano (long range fighting)

Exclusive of the above is what is known as labanang tutuhanan (actual combat).

The first (muestracion) is used in the teaching and study of the different techniques in the art of arnis. This is also the mode usually used between two skillful players.

The second (sangga at patama) is used by experienced practitioners to demonstrate the art of arnis.

The third (rompido or labanang malapitan) is used to demonstrate close quarters combat.

The fourth (labanang malayuan/larga mano) is used to demonstrate the art of arnis in long range fighting.

All of the above categories and the rest of the techniques explained in this book can be utilized by the practitioner. Their usage and application will of course depend on the individual's skill level.

Strikes and Thrusts of the Sword

(Alpabeto)

The strikes (taga) of the sword (tabak).

1. Buhat Araw (Overhead Strike)
2. Aldabis sa Ilalim (Inside Low Diagonal Upward Strike)
3. Aldabis sa Itaas (Inside High Diagonal Downward Strike)
4. Haklis/Bagsak-Salungat (Scooping Downward Strike)
5. Sablay (Low Outside Scooping/Horizontal Strike)
6. Tagang San Miguel (Outside Downward Diagonal Strike)
7. Saboy (Middle Outside Upward Diagonal Strike)
8. Tabas Talahib (Outside Horizontal Strike)
9. Tagang Alanganin (Inside Horizontal Strike)
10. Bunot Kaluban (Drawing of the Sword/Inside Upward Diagonal Strike)
11. Hulipas (Inside Diagonal Downward Strike)
12. Tigpas (Low Inside Horizontal Strike)
13. Bartikal (Backhand/Whip Strike)

The thrusts (saksak) of the sword (tabak)
1. Saksak sa gawing Kaliwa (Inside Thrust)
2. Saksan sa gawing Kanan (Outside Thrust)
3. Bulusok ng Isang Kamay (Descending/Avalanche Thrust)
4. Bulusok ng Dalawang Kamay (Double Descending/Avalanche Thrust)

Tagang Buhat Araw *(Overhead Strike)*

Buhat Araw is a vertical strike executed in the forward stance. The strike begins from the overhead position commencing downwards. Its primary target is the opponent's head.

Tagang Buhat Araw *(Overhead Strike)*

Alldabis sa Ilalim *(Inside Upward Diagonal Strike)*

The Aldabis sa Ilalim strike is executed in the forward stance with the strike originating from the low inside quadrant. This is an inside upward diagonal strike.

Alldabis sa llalim *(Inside Upward Diagonal Strike)*

Alldabis sa Itaas *(Inside Downward Diagonal Strike)*

The Aldabis sa Itaas strike is executed in the forward stance. The strike originates from the upper inside quadrant and strikes diagonally downward to the lower outside quadrant.

Alldabis sa Itaas *(Inside Downward Diagonal Strike)*

Haklis *(Scooping Strike)*

The Haklis strike is free-form and is a popular technique in the different arts and styles
of weaponry. This technique usually commences from the open/outside position and
arches downwards and upwards towards
the middle and upper parts of the
opponent's body (thigh to shoulder) with
the coordinated forward extension of the
body (similar to the Lastiko movement but
allows the rear leg to lift in forward variation). This strike is executed in the forward
stance.

Haklis *(Scooping Strike)*

Sablay   *(Low Scooping Strike)*

The Sablay strike is similar to Haklis except for the level of target areas. The prime target areas for this technique are the lower areas of the opponent's forward leg (knee to foot).

Sablay *(Low Scooping Strike)*

Tagang San Miguel *(St. Michael's Sword/Strike)*

Tagang San Miguel - (Saint Michael's Strike/Diagonal Downward Strike) This strike is executed in reverse stance with the technique commencing from the rear high outside quadrant into a downward diagonal strike. This technique targets the upper target areas of the opponent's body.

Tagang San Miguel *(St. Michael's Sword/Strike)*

Saboy   *(Outside Upward Diagonal Strike)*

Saboy - (Outside Upward Diagonal Strike)
- Counterpart to and similar in motion to
Aldabis Sa Ilalim, this technique is executed
in the reverse stance from the low outside
quadrant in an upward diagonal motion.

Saboy *(Outside Upward Diagonal Strike)*

Tabas-Talahib *(Outside Horizontal Strike)*

  Tabas Talahib - (Horizontal Strike) This strike is executed in the reverse position. The strike commences from the outside mid-level position cutting through to the inside horizontally. The primary target areas are the middle region (waist to chest) portions of the opponent's torso. This technique is also known as Planchada Abierta.

Tabas-Talahib *(Outside Horizontal Strike)*

Tagang Alanganin *(Inside Middle/ Horizontal Strike)*

Tagang Alanganin - (Inside Middle/Horizontal Strike) This strike is executed in the forward position with the strike commencing from the inside mid-level position cutting horizontally to the outside position. This is the complement of Tabas Talahib and is also known as Planchada Cerrada.

Tagang Alanganin *(Inside Middle/ Horizontal Strike)*

Bunot Kaluban   *(Drawing of the Sword)*

Bunot Kaluban - (Drawing of the Sword) Similar to Tagang Alanganin, this technique is executed in the forward stance. The technique is executed from inside to outside in an upward diagonal motion. As the name implies, the motion simulates the drawing of the sword from the scabbard. The primary target of this technique is the opponent's face or head.

Bunot Kaluban   *(Drawing of the Sword)*

Hulipas   *(Inside Transition Strike)*

Hulipas - (Transition Strike) This strike is executed in a stepping-in motion in reverse stance. The strike originates from the rear upper inside quadrant, diagonally down-ward, with the body moving in sideways. The primary target areas are the chest and shoulder areas of the opponent.

Hulipas *(Inside Transition Strike)*

Bartikal   *(Backhand/Whip Strike)*

Bartikal - (Backhand/Whip Strike) This is
an inside snap-cut strike executed in the
forward position. This strike begins from
the inside position with the edge of the
sword in an upward position (supination)
aimed at the opponent's head or chest.

Bartikal *(Backhand/Whip Strike)*

Tigpas   *(Inside Low Diagonal Upward Strike)*

Tigpas - (Inside Low Diagonal Upward Strike) This is a low upward diagonal strike executed in forward stance with the strike commencing from the inside lower quadrant moving diagonally upwards to outside lower quadrant. The target areas are the lower region (foot to knee) of the opponent's forward leg.

Tigpas   *(Inside Low Diagonal Upward Strike)*

Saksak sa gawing Kaliwa *(Inside Sword Thrust)*

Saksak sa gawing Kaliwa (Inside Sword Thrust) This is an inside thrust executed with the palm-up in forward stance. The thrust is delivered at chest height while the secondary weapon is held up high in a ready support position. The target is the general torso area.

Note: In some systems, this particular inside thrust is referred to as: a) Cerrada Sungkite or Tusok/Saksak Cerrada (both meaning Inside Thrust) ; b) Ang Makata (The Poet).

Saksak sa gawing Kanan *(Outside Sword Thrust)*

Saksak sa gawing Kanan (Outside Sword Thrust). This is an outside thrust executed from the right side of the body, chest height, palm down, with the left foot in front (reverse forward stance). The primary target area is the chest area of the opponent .

Note: In other systems, this particular thrust when used in conjunction with the parrying left hand or secondary weapon is known as either Tulay (parry is above the thrust) or Lagusan (parry is below the thrust).

Bulusok ng Dalawang Kamay

(Double Descending/Avalanche Thrust)

Bulusok ng Dalawang Kamay (Double Descending/Avalance Thrust Technique)

Bulusok is a descending thrust executed from shoulder or higher position, crossing outside to inside, with the body in a lateral position, angled and leaned into a pronounced sidewards position in reverse stance. The primary target area is the opponent's chest.

Note: A requisite technique or parry prior to this movement is the Palis (sweeping parry) or Hataw (beat) which dislodges the opponent's weapon(s) from the center/defense line and opens up the central target area for the twin thrust technique.

Techniques of the Dagger

The Thrust with the Dagger (Balaraw/Daga).

The use of the dagger is free form and may come from any direction but all thrusts must concentrate on the body of the opponent. The dagger according to the art of arnis, must be utilized in the same speed and fashion as the tabak/espada and must assist in any form of blocking when needed (i.e, Sikwat, Palis, Tabig, Salikop, Tulay and Lagusan, etc., techniques).

Lagusan *(Tunnel Thrust)*

Thrust with the dagger from the outside in reverse stance. The primary weapon is used to parry and create an opening for the execution of a thrust with the dagger. The thrust is delivered either from a Lagusan (Tunnel Thrust) technique with the sword pointing to the ground, Tusok-Nakaw (Criss-Cross Thrust), a technique similar to Lagusan but with the sword pointing upward or Tulay (Bridge Thrust) with the sword parrying above the dagger arm.

In Lagusan, the dagger passes over and above the sword arm, which executed a cross-parry against a thrust or a low strike. This primary weapon parry is the first movement of the Bunot Kaluban technique. The body is positioned sideways with the right foot leading after having executed a forward diagonal side-step to avoid the opponent's thrust.

Ang Makata *(The Poet)*

A lunge thrust with the dagger executed with a simultaneous step/lunge. This position is similar to the Saksak ng Kanan - Loob (Inside Thrust) technique with the primary weapon. Executed palm-up for maximum extension, this thrust technique is commonly known as Ang Makata (The Poet).

Sima-Tulay *(Scythe Parry and Thrust)*

Thrust with the dagger in reverse stance. This technique is usually seen as the final stage of a Sima-Tulay or Sumbrada-Sungkite technique. The position of the dagger is angled in such a manner that the opponent's perspective of the weapon's true length and distance is deceived.

This may result from either executing an outside scythe parry (Sima) or a Sumbrada (Roof Block) with the Tabak followed immediately by a thrust with the dagger.

Tusok-Fraile *(Friar's Thrust)*

A counter-thrust with the dagger after an overhead parry or feint. The primary weapon is held in Fraile (Friar's blessing) position while simultaneously lunging forward to deliver a thrust with the dagger. This technique is known by a variety of names such as Tusok-Sinalakot, Tusok-Sumbrada, Sungkite-Sumbrada, Tusok-Fraile, etc.

Classic **ARNIS**

The Foundation Drills
(Mga Abakada)

Possibly one of the mysteries and secrets of Placido Yambao's book is his selection and presentation of the 10 Foundation (abakada) drills. The foundation drills represent the complete set of techniques executed by the initiating/attacking participant in each of the forms (regla/abakada ng taga at sangga) performed without a partner. This in itself is not unusual.

What makes this intriguing is that:
1. The corresponding set of techniques of the defending/receiving participant in each of the forms (regla) are not performed nor mentioned as a separate drill (abakada).
2. The best and most powerful techniques and combinations can be found in the defender's/receiver's repertoire.

In the supplementary materials, you will find the Sinawali techniques and drills that expand and explain the techniques of the defending/receiving participant. Familiarity and skill with these techniques are requisite to performing the final and complete drills. Without this knowledge, the gaps that Yambao inadvertently (or possibly intentionally) left will continue to puzzle and prevent the reader from appreciating this legacy.

The Foundation Drills for Strikes as well as the Foundation Drills for the Blocks can be performed by following the steps/actions as prescribed in the corresponding column for the attacker (A) and the defender (D). These can be treated, as Yambao intended, as separate forms. However, it is during the execution of the complete drill and the ensuing interaction between the offense and defense that the precision and strategy behind the concept can be truly appreciated.

From the original edition:

All the positions, sequence and combinations of hand, foot, and body movements, including the stances and techniques that are demonstrated and exemplified in this book are derived from the Foundation (Techniques) of the Five Strikes, from the drills 1, 2, 3, and 4. Only after understanding and mastering all the steps and concepts in these series can one claim having achieved and mastered the Art and Foundation of the Five Strikes.

Classic **ARNIS**

Strikes and Blocks 1

(Blg. 1 - Taga at Sangga sa Abakada ng LimangTaga)

Placido Yambao and Luis Cruz

1. Taga at Sangga sa Abakada ng Limang Taga
(Strikes and Blocks - Five Strikes Set - Drill I)

Actions:

	Attacker	Defender
1.	Buhat Araw	Sanggang Papalis
2.	Aldabis Sa Ilalim	Haklis
	2.1 Sikwat Ng Kaliwa	
3.	Aldabis Sa Itaas	Sanggang Payong
	3.1 Saksak Ng Kaliwa	Bulalakaw
4.	Tagang Saboy	Sanggang Salikop
	4.1 Saksak Ng Kaliwa	Tiklop-Pana
5.	Tagang San Miguel	Bulalakaw

Strikes and Blocks 1
(Blg. 1 - Taga at Sangga sa Abakada ng LimangTaga)

A (1): Execute an overhead downward strike (Buhat Araw) in right forward stance.

D (1): Step diagonally forward with the right foot and intercept the incoming strike with a Sanggang Papalis, gliding with and redirecting the strike to the far right away from the center. Execute the Sanggang Papalis commencing from the waist level going slightly diagonally upward and beyond the centerline and at eye level. The dagger follows the movement and direction of the parry, acting as an auxiliary and reinforcing tool and is chambered near the right upper arm.

A (2): Convert the deflected strike into an inside upward diagonal strike (Aldabis sa Ilalim) aiming for D's forward leg.

D (2): Withdraw the right foot at the same time following (and controlling the attacker's sword) with an outside downward diagonal strike (Haklis). In actual combat, the Haklis should strike at the attacker's forearm.

A (2.1): Use the dagger to execute an intercept technique (Sikwat ng Kaliwa) under the right arm to check and control the defender's sword. Withdraw and chamber the sword over the left arm with the tip pointing downwards.

76

Strikes and Blocks 1

(Blg. 1 - Taga at Sangga sa Abakada ng LimangTaga)

A (3): Execute an inside downward strike (Aldabis sa Itaas), aiming for the defender's head.

> D (3): Execute a roof block (Sanggang Payong) in a Salibas sword over dagger technique to protect against the attacker's strike at the same time checking the attacker's weapon hand with the dagger. Refer to Salibas-Salisok drills for the simultaneous outward circular motion of the sword and dagger.

A (3.1): Execute a Saksak ng Kaliwa - a lunging thrust (stepping forward with the left foot) with the dagger at the defender's chest.

> D (3.1): Parry and counter-attack using the Bulalakaw technique.
>
> The three stages of the Bulalakaw technique are detailed as steps D(3.1a) thru D(3.1c).
>
> D (3.1a): Vertical parry with the sword. Note the inside chambered position of the defender's dagger.

> D (3.1b): Replace the sword that deflected and controlled the attacker's weapon with the dagger. The defender's sword is withdrawn and chambered below the dagger arm.

Strikes and Blocks 1
(Blg. 1 - Taga at Sangga sa Abakada ng LimangTaga)

D (3.1c): Keeping control of the attacker's weapon with the dagger, whip out the chambered sword to deliver a strike at the attacker's chest.

Steps D (3.1a) thru to D (3.1c) are the elements of the Bulalakaw technique.

A(4): Execute a low outside upward diagonal strike (Tagang Saboy) at the same time withdrawing the dagger.

D (4): Intercept and block the Saboy strike with an augmented block (Sanggang Salikop).

Strikes and Blocks 1

(Blg. 1 - Taga at Sangga sa Abakada ng LimangTaga)

A(4.1): Deliver a thrust (Saksak ng Kaliwa) with the dagger at the defender's chest and pull the sword back to the low right rear position.

D (4.1): Parry and counter-attack by continuing the Sanggang Salikop into Tiklop-Pana.

D (4.1a) Chamber the sword over the dagger to create a high reverse augmented block and deflect the attacker's thrust.

D (4.1b) Transfer control to the dagger from underneath the sword arm. Deliver a strike with the sword at the attacker's head.

Steps D (4.1a) thru to D (4.1b) are the elements of the Tiklop-Pana technique.

A(5): Execute an outside downward diagonal strike (Tagang San Miguel).

D (5): Parry and counter-attack using the tri-step Bulalakaw technique.
The three stages of the Bulalakaw technique are detailed as steps D(5a) thru D(5c).

D (5a): Side-step and execute a vertical parry with the sword. Note the inside chambered position of the defender's dagger.

Strikes and Blocks 1
(Blg. 1 - Taga at Sangga sa Abakada ng LimangTaga)

D (5b): Replace the sword check on the attacker's weapon with the dagger. The sword is chambered below the dagger arm.

D (5c): Keeping control of the attacker's sword with the dagger, whip out the chambered sword to deliver a strike at the attacker's chest.

Steps D (5a) thru to D (5c) are the elements of the Bulalakaw technique.

Strikes and Blocks 2
(Blg. 2 - Taga at Sangga sa Abakada ng LimangTaga)

Placido Yambao and Luis Cruz

2. Taga at Sangga sa Abakada ng Limang Taga
(Strikes and Blocks - Five Strikes Set - Drill 2)
Anyong Malayuan   *(Long Range Form)*

Attacker	*Defender*
1. Tagang San Miguel	Aldabis sa Itaas
2. Aldabis sa Ilalim	Haklis
2.1 Saksak ng Kaliwa	Bulalakaw
3. Saboy	Sanngang Salikop
3.1 Saksak ng Kaliwa	Tiklop-Pana
4. Bulusok ng Tabak at Balaraw	Tiklop-Pana
5. Haklis	Tagang Pasumala

From the original manuscript:
The art of the sword and dagger as demonstrated in this drill is performed with full control and no actual strike or hit ever touching any of the practitioners. The defense (D) when executing the full technique, performs the action above or beyond the actual targets. The same holds true for the offense (A). If under any circumstance a strike may hit the partner, restrain and control the movement so that it stops before contact or adjust it slightly so that it brushes past the target and injury is prevented.

Strikes and Blocks 2
(Blg. 2 - Taga at Sangga sa Abakada ng LimangTaga)

A (1): Execute, with the sword , a Tagang San Miguel strike in left forward stance. The left hand, which holds the dagger is held towards the left rear, mid level,with the tip pointing upward.

D (1): Step diagonally forward with the right foot and intercept the incoming strike with an Aldabis sa Itaas. The block begins from the inside and redirects the attack to the far right away from the center. The dagger follows the movement and direction of the parry and is chambered under the right upper arm.

A (2): Convert the deflected strike into an Aldabis sa Ilalim aiming for D's near leg. The dagger is held in upper left corner.

D (2): Withdraw the right foot and at the same time following and controlling the attacker's sword with a Haklis. In actual combat, the Haklis should strike at the attacker's forearm.

A (2.1): Execute a lunging thrust (stepping forward with the left foot) with the dagger at the defender's chest.

D (2.1): Step back with the left foot and parry and counter-attack using the Bulalakaw technique.
The three stages of the Bulalakaw technique are detailed as steps B (2.1a) thru B (2.1c).

D (2.1a): Vertical parry with the sword. Note the inside chambered position of the defender's dagger.

82

Strikes and Blocks 2
(Blg. 2 - Taga at Sangga sa Abakada ng LimangTaga)

D (2.1b): Replace the sword check on the attacker's weapon with the dagger. The sword is chambered below the dagger arm.

D (2.1c): Keeping control of the attacker's dagger with the dagger, whip out the chambered sword and deliver an upward diagonal strike at the attacker's chest.

Steps D (2.1a) thru to D (2.1c) are the elements of the Bulalakaw technique.

Strikes and Blocks 2
(Blg. 2 - Taga at Sangga sa Abakada ng LimangTaga)

A (3): Execute a Saboy strike at the same time withdrawing the dagger.

    D (3): Intercept and block the Saboy strike with a Sanggang Salikop.

A (3.1): Deliver a thrust with the dagger at the defender's chest.

    D (3.1a): Parry and counter-attack by converting the Sanggang-Salikop into Tiklop-Pana. Deflect the thrust with a high reverse augmented block using a sword and dagger combination.

    D (3.1b): Replace the parrying and controlling weapon with the dagger and chamber the sword over the left arm. Keep control of the attacker's weapon with the dagger.

    D (3.1c): Keeping control of the attacker's thrusting weapon with the dagger, release the chambered sword and deliver an Aldabis sa Itaas strike at the attacker's head.

Strikes and Blocks 2
(Blg. 2 - Taga at Sangga sa Abakada ng LimangTaga)

Steps D (3.1a) thru to D (3.1c) are the elements of theTiklop-Pana technique.

A(4): Execute a Bulusok ng Dalawang Kamay.

D (3.1a): Parry and counter-attack with the augmented block of Tiklop-Pana. Deflect the thrust with the sword and dagger combination (high reverse augmented block).

D (3.1b) Switch the controlling weapon and chamber the sword over the left arm, keeping check of the attacker's weapons with the dagger.

Strikes and Blocks 2
(Blg. 2 - Taga at Sangga sa Abakada ng LimangTaga)

D (4.1c): Keeping control of the attacker's weapons with the dagger, strike out with the chambered sword and deliver a Hulipas strike at the attacker's head.

Steps D (4.1a) thru to D (4.1c) are the elements of the Tiklop-Pana technique.

A (5): Execute a Haklis strike at the same time withdrawing the left leg.

D (5): Parry the attack with a Tagang Pasumala, stepping forward with the left foot. Swing the dagger to the left ready position.

Strikes and Blocks 3

(Blg. 3 - Taga at Sangga sa Abakada ng LimangTaga)

Luis Cruz and Placido Yambao

3. Taga at Sangga ng Abakada ng Limang Taga
   (Strikes and Blocks - Five Strikes Set - Drill 3)

Attacker	*Defender*
1. Buhat Araw	Aldabis Sa Itaas
	Buhat Araw
2. Aldabis sa Ilalim	Salibas sa Ibaba
	Tagang San Miguel
2.1 Saksak ng Kaliwa	Bulalakaw
3. Saboy	Tagang Papalis
	Sikwat ng Kaliwa
	Aldabis sa Itaas
3.1 Saksak ng Kaliwa	Bulalakaw
4. Bulusok ng Dalawang Kamay	Bulalakaw
5. Haklis	Bulalakaw

Strikes and Blocks 3
(Blg. 3 - Taga at Sangga sa Abakada ng LimangTaga)

A (1): Execute a Buhat Araw strike in right forward stance.

D (1a): Execute an Aldabis sa Itaas (using Salibas sword over dagger technique) to protect against the Buhat Araw strike. In combat the dagger is used to check the attacker's weapon hand. Refer to Salibas-Salisok technique for the simultaneous outward circular motion of the sword and dagger.

D (1b): Disengage the sword and deliver a Buhat-Araw strike. Use the dagger to keep control of the opponent's sword.

A (2): Deliver an Aldabis sa Ilalim strike.

D (2a): Step back with the right foot to avoid the attacker's strike. Execute a low outward circular parry (Salibas dagger over sword technique) to intercept the attack.

Strikes and Blocks 3
(Blg. 3 - Taga at Sangga sa Abakada ng LimangTaga)

D (2b): Continue the outward and upward swing of the sword and then deliver an outside descending diagonal strike (Tagang San Miguel).

A (2.1): Execute a lunging thrust (stepping forward with the left foot) with the dagger (Saksak ng Kaliwa) at the defender's chest.

D (2.1): Parry and counter-attack using the Bulalakaw technique.
The three stages of the Bulalakaw technique are detailed as steps D (2.1a) thru D (2.1c).

D (2.1a): Step back with the left foot and execute a vertical parry with the sword.

D (2.1b): Replace the sword check on the attacker's weapon with the dagger. The sword is chambered below the dagger arm.

Strikes and Blocks 3

(Blg. 3 - Taga at Sangga sa Abakada ng LimangTaga)

D (2.1c): Keeping control of the attacker's thrusting weapon with the dagger, unleash the chambered sword and deliver a strike at the attacker's chest.

Steps D (2.1a) thru to D (2.1c) are the elements of the Bulalakaw technique.

A (3): Execute a Saboy strike at the same time withdrawing the dagger.

D (3a): Execute a Tagang Papalis, leaning the body towards the rear (Lastiko movement).

D (3b): Switch and replace the parry with the dagger and chamber the sword over the dagger arm.

Strikes and Blocks 3
(Blg. 3 - Taga at Sangga sa Abakada ng LimangTaga)

D (3c): Deliver an Aldabis sa Itaas at the attacker's head.

Steps D (3a) thru to D (3c) are the elements of the Palis-Aldabis technique.

A (3.1): Execute a thrust (Saksak ng Kaliwa) to the body with the dagger.

D (3.1): Parry and counter-attack using the Bulalakaw technique.
The three stages of the Bulalakaw technique are detailed as steps D (3.1a) thru D (3.1c).

D (3.1a): Vertical parry with the sword. Note the inside chambered position of the defender's dagger.

D (3.1b): Replace the sword check on the attacker's weapon with the dagger. The sword is chambered under the dagger arm.

Strikes and Blocks 3
(Blg. 3 - Taga at Sangga sa Abakada ng LimangTaga)

D (3.1c): Keeping control of the attacker's extended weapon with the dagger, unleash the chambered sword and deliver an upward diagonal strike at the attacker's chest.

Steps D (3.1a) thru to D (3.1c) are the elements of the Bulalakaw technique.

A (4) Execute a double descending thrust (Bulusok ng Dalawang Kamay) with the sword and dagger.

D (4.1): Parry and counter-attack using the Bulalakaw technique.
The three stages of the Bulalakaw technique are detailed as steps D (4.1a) thru D (4.1c).

D (4.1a): Vertical parry with the sword. Note the pre-established position of the defender's dagger in anticipation of the weapons switch.

D (4.1b): Replace the sword check on the attacker's weapon with the dagger. Chamber the sword below the dagger arm.

Strikes and Blocks 3

(Blg. 3 - Taga at Sangga sa Abakada ng LimangTaga)

D (4.1c): Keeping control of the attacker's weapon with the dagger, release the chambered sword and deliver an upward diagonal strike at the attacker's chest.

A (5): Execute a horizontal (Haklis) strike at the same time stepping back with the left foot.

D (5.1):Step forward with the left foot and parry and counter-attack using the Bulalakaw technique.

The three stages of the Bulalakaw technique are detailed as steps D (5.1a) thru D (5.1c).

D (5.1a): Vertical parry with the sword. Note the inside chambered position of the defender's dagger.

Strikes and Blocks 3
(Blg. 3 - Taga at Sangga sa Abakada ng LimangTaga)

D (5.1b): Replace the sword check on the attacker's weapon with the dagger. The sword is chambered under the dagger arm.

D (5.1c): Keeping control of the attacker's sword with the dagger, whip out the chambered sword and deliver an upward diagonal strike at the attacker's chest.

From the original manuscript:
The drills of the five strikes that involve blocks and strikes serve to illustrate the techniques of offense and defense. It also serves to highlight the primary targets. This literature will never be able to accurately demonstrate all the requisite defensive movements for either party. Such knowledge and expertise can only be gained through experience and dedication.

Strikes and Blocks 4

(Blg. 4 - Taga at Sangga sa Abakada ng Apat na Taga)

Placido Yambao and Luis Cruz

4. Taga at Sangga ng Abakada ng Apat na Taga
   (Strikes and Blocks - Four Step Set - Drill - 4)

Attacker	*Defender*
1. Buhat Araw	Tabig ng Tabak (Salibas)
2. Aldabis sa Ilalim	Salibas, Ibaba
2.1 Saksak ng Balaraw	Tiklop-Pana
3. Saboy	Kambal-Bagsak
3.1 Saksak ng Balaraw	Tiklop-Pana
4. Tagang San Miguel	Bulalakaw
4.1 Saksak ng Balaraw	Sikwat-Abaniko

Strikes and Blocks 4

(Blg. 4 - Taga at Sangga sa Abakada ng Apat na Taga)

A (1): Execute a Buhat Araw strike in right forward stance. The left hand, which holds the dagger, is held towards the left rear, mid level, with the tip pointing upward.

D (1): Step diagonally forward with the left foot and execute a mid-level parry (Tabig ng Tabak) using a dagger over sword variation of the Salibas movement. Keep the dagger in a protective Sumbrada position.

A (2): Convert the deflected strike into an Aldabis sa Ilalim aiming for D's forward leg.

D (2): Intercept the incoming strike with a low level parry using Salibas dagger over sword movement. Make sure the sword stops the progress of the attacker's sword.

D: Use the dagger to check and trap the opponent's weapon hand.

Strikes and Blocks 4

(Blg. 4 - Taga at Sangga sa Abakada ng Apat na Taga)

A (2.1): Execute a thrust (Saksak ng Balaraw) to the body with the dagger.

D (2.1): Parry and counter-attack using the Tiklop-Pana technique.

The three stages of the Tiklop-Pana technique are detailed as steps D (2.1a) thru D (2.1c).

D (2.1a): Execute a sweeping hanging parry with the sword. Note the inside chambered position of the defender's dagger.

D (2.1b): Replace the sword check on the attacker's weapon with the dagger. The sword is chambered over the dagger arm.

D (2.1c): Keeping control of the attacker's extended weapon with the dagger, unleash the chambered sword and deliver a downward diagonal strike at the attacker's head.

Strikes and Blocks 4

(Blg. 4 - Taga at Sangga sa Abakada ng Apat na Taga)

A (3): Execute a Saboy strike at the same time withdrawing the dagger.

D (3): Execute a double downward block (Kambal-Bagsak) to stop the attacker's strike. Position the dagger to intercept the attacker's weapon hand.

A (3.1): Execute a thrust (Saksak ng Balaraw) to the body with the dagger.

D (3.1): Parry and counter-attack using the Tiklop-Pana technique.

The three stages of the Tiklop-Pana technique are detailed as steps D (3.1a) thru D (3.1c).

D (3.1a): Execute a sweeping hanging parry with the sword. Note the inside chambered position of the defender's dagger.

D (3.1b): Replace the sword check on the attacker's weapon with the dagger. The sword is chambered over the dagger arm.

Strikes and Blocks 4

(Blg. 4 - Taga at Sangga sa Abakada ng Apat na Taga)

D (3.1c): Keeping control of the attacker's extended weapon with the dagger, unleash the chambered sword and deliver a downward diagonal strike at the attacker's head.

Steps D (3.1a) thru to D (3.1c) are the elements of the Tiklop- Pana technique.

A (4): Deliver a downward diagonal strike (Tagang San Miguel) at the defender's head.

D (4.1): Parry and counter-attack using the Bulalakaw technique.
The three stages of the Bulalakaw technique are detailed as steps D (4.1a) thru D (4.1c).

D (4.1a): Vertical parry with the sword. Note the inside chambered position of the defender's dagger.

D (4.1b): Replace the sword check on the attacker's weapon with the dagger. The sword is chambered under the dagger arm.

99

Strikes and Blocks 4
(Blg. 4 - Taga at Sangga sa Abakada ng Apat na Taga)

D (4.1c): Keeping control of the attacker's extended weapon with the dagger, unleash the chambered sword and deliver an upward diagonal strike at the attacker's chest.

A (4.1): Thrust with the dagger (Saksak ng Balaraw) at the defender's chest.

D (4.1): Execute a simultaneous parry and strike technique (Sikwat-Abaniko). Parry the thrust with a downward circular motion of the dagger while delivering a strike to opponent's head with the sword. This technique can be found in the Putakti (The Hornet) drill and is the last stage in the tri-step drill.

From the original manuscript:
This drill is comprised of four strikes with the sword and three thrusts with the dagger. The combinations in this drill may be used for practice or in actual close quarters combat.

Strikes and Blocks 5
(Blg. 5 - Taga at Sangga sa Abakada ng Anim na Taga)

Buenaventura Mirafuente and Placido Yambao

5. Taga at Sangga ng Abakada ng Anim na Taga
   (Strikes and Blocks - Six Strikes Set – Drill 5)

Attacker	*Defender*
1. Buhat Araw	Palis-Kaluban
2. Aldabis sa Ilalim	Salibas sa Ibaba
2.1 Saksak ng Kaliwa	Palis-Kaluban
3. Aldabis sa Itaas	Sanggang-Payong (Salibas)
3.1 Saksak ng Kaliwa	Bulalakaw
4. Saboy	Salikop-Saliwa
4.1 Saksak ng Kaliwa	Makata
5. Saksak ng Kanan (Tabak)	Palis ng Tabak
(Salisi ang Paa)	
6. Haklis	Palis ng Dalawang Kamay
	Tagang San Miguel

From the original manuscript:
Note: The drill of the six strikes can be classified as controlling or "rumpido" - as it was called in the past. This was due to the fact that the drill includes footwork and body mechanics that tend to pressure and control the opponent. In addition, the strategy and techniques used have combinations of defense, control of the opponent's weapon, and specific targets.

Strikes and Blocks 5
(Blg. 5 - Taga at Sangga sa Abakada ng Anim na Taga)

A (1): Execute a downward strike (Buhat Araw) strike.

D (1): Execute a Palis-Kaluban parry. Palis-Kaluban is detailed in steps D (1a) to D (1b).

D (1a): Parry the Buhat Araw strike with the sword in a sweeping left to right motion. Prepare and position the dagger inside and over the sword arm to support and replace the sword.

D (1b): Use the dagger to check the opponent's weapon arm. The sword is held in the scabbard (kaluban) position.

A (2): Disengage the sword and execute an inside upward diagonal strike (Aldabis sa Ilalim).

D (2): Step back with the right foot to avoid the incoming strike at the same time execute a low Salibas (dagger over sword) parry and check technique.

Strikes and Blocks 5

(Blg. 5 - Taga at Sangga sa Abakada ng Anim na Taga)

A (2.1): Execute a thrust with the dagger.

D (2.1): Execute a Palis-Kaluban parry. Palis-Kaluban is detailed in steps D (2.1a) to D (2.1b).

D (2.1a): Parry the thrust with the sword in a sweeping left to right motion. Prepare and position the dagger inside and over the sword arm to support and replace the sword.

D (2.1b): Use the dagger to check the opponent's weapon arm. The sword is held in the scabbard (kaluban) position.

A (3): Step back with the left foot and execute an inside downward diagonal (Aldabis sa Itaas) strike.

D (3): Step diagonally forward with the right foot and execute a roof block (Sanggang Payong) to protect against the Aldabis sa Itaas at the same time checking the attacker's weapon hand with the dagger. Use the high Salibas sword over dagger technique.

103

Strikes and Blocks 5
(Blg. 5 - Taga at Sangga sa Abakada ng Anim na Taga)

A (3.1): Step forward with the left foot and execute a thrust (Saksak ng Kaliwa) with dagger.

D (3.1): Parry and counter-attack using the Bulalakaw technique.

The three stages of the Bulalakaw technique are detailed as step D (3.1a) thru D (3.1c).

D (3.1a): Vertical parry with the sword. Note the inside chambered position of the defender's dagger.

D (3.1b): Replace the sword that is controlling the attacker's weapon with the dagger. The defender's sword is then chambered below the dagger arm.

D (3.1c): Keeping control of the attacker's thrusting weapon with the dagger, release the chambered sword to deliver a strike at the attacker's chest.

Strikes and Blocks 5
(Blg. 5 - Taga at Sangga sa Abakada ng Anim na Taga)

A (4): Deliver an outside upward diagonal (Saboy) strike.

> D (4): Intercept and block the Saboy strike with a Salikop-Saliwa.
> Note: Salikop-Saliwa is an augmented block performed in reverse layer position. In this particular case the dagger is positioned inside and the sword is on the outside.

A (4.1): Execute a thrust (Saksak ng Kaliwa) with the dagger.

> D (4.1): Parry the thrust with the dagger in an upward fan motion. At the same time extend the sword into a thrust towards the attacker's chest. This particular combination technique is collectively known as Makata (The Poet).

A (5): Disengage and withdraw the dagger and execute an outside thrust with the sword (Saksak ng Kanan).

> D (5.1): Parry the thrust with the sword in a sweeping (Papalis) left to right motion.

Strikes and Blocks 5

(Blg. 5 - Taga at Sangga sa Abakada ng Anim na Taga)

A (6): Turn the sword in supination and execute a Haklis strike at the same time taking a step back with the left foot.

D (6a): Step forward with the left foot and execute a double right to left parry, keeping the attacker's weapon hand in check with the dagger.

D (6b): Execute a downward diagonal (San Miguel) strike at the attacker's head.

Strikes and Blocks 6

(Blg. 6 - Taga at Sangga sa Abakada ng Apat na Taga)

Placido Yambao and Buenaventura Mirafuente

6. Taga at Sangga ng Abakada ng Apat na Taga
(Strikes and Blocks - Four Step Set – Drill 6)

Attacker	*Defender*
1. Buhat Araw	Sanggang-Taga (Salibas)
2. Aldabis sa Ilalim	
	Tagang Papalis
	Tagang Pahulipas
2.1 Saksak ng Kaliwa	Bulalakaw
3. Saboy	Tagang Papalis
	Tagang San Miguel
4. Bartikal	Bulalakaw

Strikes and Blocks 6
(Blg. 6 - Taga at Sangga sa Abakada ng Apat na Taga)

A (1): Execute an overhead (Buhat Araw) strike.

D (1): Step forward with the right foot diagonally crossing the center-line to the opponent's right. Execute a Sanggang-Taga (Salibas dagger over sword technique), striking at the opponent's sword arm.

A (2): Execute an inside upward diagonal (Aldabis sa Ilalim) strike.

D (2a): Follow sword with sword (Tagang Papalis) the opponent's Aldabis sa Ilalim, withdrawing the right foot to avoid the opponent's sword.

D (2b): Intercept and control the opponent's sword with the dagger (Sikwat ng Kaliwa) and chamber the sword over the left arm in preparation for a counter-strike.

Strikes and Blocks 6

(Blg. 6 - Taga at Sangga sa Abakada ng Apat na Taga)

D (2c): Deliver a Tagang Pahulipas at the opponent's chest.

The Tagang Pahulipas should be performed as one continuous motion from strike and back to ready position.

Steps D (2a) thru to D (2c) are the elements of a technique collectively known as Sikwat-Aldabis.

A (2.1): Lunge forward with the left foot and deliver a thrust with the dagger (Saksak ng Kaliwa).

D (2.1): Parry and counter-attack using the Bulalakaw technique.

The three stages of the Bulalakaw technique are detailed as step D (2.1a) thru D (2.1c).

D (2.1a): Vertical parry with the sword. Note the inside chambered position of the defender's dagger.

Strikes and Blocks 6
(Blg. 6 - Taga at Sangga sa Abakada ng Apat na Taga)

D (2.1b): Replace the sword that is controlling the attacker's weapon with the dagger. The defender's sword is then chambered below the dagger arm.

D (2.1c): Keeping control of the attacker's thrusting weapon with the dagger, release the chambered sword to deliver a strike at the attacker's chest.

Steps D (2.1a) thru to D (2.1c) are the elements of the Bulalakaw technique.

A (3): Deliver an outside low upward diagonal (Saboy) strike.

D (3.1a): Take a step back with the right foot and swing the sword to the inside in a downward diagonal motion to deflect and sweep (Tagang Papalis) the opponent's sword.

Strikes and Blocks 6
(Blg. 6 - Taga at Sangga sa Abakada ng Apat na Taga)

D (3.1b): Use the momentum of the deflecting motion to continue to return the swing into an outside downward diagonal strike (Tagang San Miguel).

A (4): Deliver a reverse vertical snap thrust with the sword (Bartikal) while stepping back with the left foot.

D (4): Parry and counter-attack using the Bulalakaw technique.
The three stages of the Bulalakaw technique are detailed as stepD (4a) thru D (4c).

D (4a): Vertical parry with the sword. Note the inside chambered position of the defender's dagger.

D (4b): Replace the sword that is controlling the attacker's weapon with the dagger. The defender's sword is then chambered below the dagger arm.

Strikes and Blocks 6
(Blg. 6 - Taga at Sangga sa Abakada ng Apat na Taga)

D (4c): Keeping control of the attacker's thrusting weapon with the dagger, release the chambered sword to deliver a strike at the attacker's chest.

The Tagang Pahulipas should be performed as one continuous motion from strike and back to ready position.

Strikes and Blocks 7

(Blg. 7 - Taga at Sangga sa Abakada ng Pitong Taga)

Buenaventura Mirafuente and Placido Yambao

7. Taga at Sangga ng Abakada ng Pitong Taga

(Strikes and Blocks - Seven Step Set – Drill 7)

Attacker	*Defender*
1. Buhat Araw	Tagang San Miguel
	Tagang Alanganin
2. Aldabis sa Ilalim	Salibas
	Tagang San Miguel
2.1 Saksak ng Balaraw)	Bulalakaw
3. Saboy	Kambal-Bagsak
3.1 Saksak ng Kaliwa	Tabig ng Kaliwa
4. Tabas Talahib	Tagang Papalis
5. Tagang Alanganin	Salibas
6. Bulusok ng Dalawang Kamay	Sanggang Papalis
7. Haklis	Sanggang Papalis
	Haklis

Strikes and Blocks 7
(Blg. 7 - Taga at Sangga sa Abakada ng Pitong Taga)

A (1): Execute a downward vertical strike (Buhat Araw) with the sword, right foot forward. Keep the dagger in the low left rear position.

D (1a): Step forward with the left foot and block the Buhat Araw strike with a Tagang San Miguel. The dagger is kept overhead as a secondary check against the opponent's sword.

D (1b): Continue the downward diagonal motion to pass beyond the opponent's sword and slash back in a horizontal motion (Tagang Alanganin) at the opponent's exposed right arm or side.

A (2): Shift forward with the right foot and deliver an inside upward diagonal strike (Aldabis sa Ilalim) . Raise the dagger up to the the left shoulder level.

D (2): Execute a Salibas sword over dagger , taking a step back with the left foot to allow the opponent's sword to pass.

Strikes and Blocks 7
(Blg. 7 - Taga at Sangga sa Abakada ng Pitong Taga)

D (2b): Keeping the opponent's sword in check with the dagger, execute an outside downward diagonal (Tagang San Miguel) strike.

A (2.1): Step forward with the left foot and deliver a thrust with the dagger (Saksak ng Kaliwa) at the same withdrawing the sword upwards to the right.

D (2.1): Parry and counter-attack using the Bulalakaw technique.
The three stages of the Bulalakaw technique are detailed as stepD (2.1a) thru D (2.1c).

D (2.1a): Vertical parry with the sword. Note the inside chambered position of the defender's dagger.

D (2.1b): Replace the sword that is controlling the attacker's weapon with the dagger. The defender's sword is then chambered below the dagger arm.

Strikes and Blocks 7
(Blg. 7 - Taga at Sangga sa Abakada ng Pitong Taga)

D (1.2c): Keeping control of the attacker's thrusting weapon with the dagger, release the chambered sword to deliver a strike at the attacker's chest.

Steps D (2.1a) thru to D (2.1c) are the elements of the Bulalakaw technique.

A (3): Withdraw the dagger to the left rear and deliver an outside upward diagonal strike (Saboy).

D (3): Execute a Kambal Bagsak (Concierto) against the Saboy, the sword striking the opponent's sword arm and the dagger intercepting the Saboy strike.

A (3.1): Parry the opponent's sword using the dagger in a left to right motion at the same time withdrawing the sword back to the rear.

Strikes and Blocks 7
(Blg. 7 - Taga at Sangga sa Abakada ng Pitong Taga)

D (3.1) : Release the opponent's control on the sword by disengaging the attacker's dagger with the dagger in a right to left motion (Salibas sword over dagger). Extract the sword back to the outside ready position.

A (4): Execute an outside horizontal strike (Tabas-Talahib) simultaneously stepping back with the left foot.

D (4): Shift the body over the rear leg and execute a Tagang Papalis.

A (5): Deliver an inside horizontal strike (Tagang Alanganin) at the end take a step forward with the left foot.

D (5): Step back with the right foot and execute a Salibas sword over dagger technique resulting in a Sanggang Papalis with a dagger check , bringing the body over the rear leg.

117

Strikes and Blocks 7
(Blg. 7 - Taga at Sangga sa Abakada ng Pitong Taga)

A (6): Lean sideways and forward to deliver a double descending thrust (Bulusok ng Dalawang Kamay).

D (6): Step back with the left foot and execute a double sweeping (Sanggang Papalis) parry.

A (7): Step back with the left foot and deliver an outside diagonal strike (Haklis).

D (7a): Step forward with the left and execute a left to right sweeping (Sanggang Papalis) parry.

D (7b): Step forward with the right foot and swing the sword into an outside diagonal (Haklis) strike.

Strikes and Blocks 8
(Blg. 8 - Taga at Sangga sa Abakada ng Labindalawang Taga)

Placido Yambao and Buenaventura Mirafuente

8. Taga at Sangga ng Abakada ng Labindalawang Taga
(Strikes and Blocks - Twelve Step Set - Drill 8)

Attacker	*Defender*
1. Buhat Araw	Lagusan
2. Aldabis sa Ilalim	Salibas
2.1 Saksak ng Kaliwa	Palis-Kaluban
3. Aldabis sa Itaas/Bagsak Salungat	
	Sanggang Payong
3.1 Saksak ng Kaliwa	Bulalakaw
4. Saboy	Kambal-Bagsak
4.1 Saksak ng Kaliwa	Palis-Kaluban
5. Tagang San Miguel	Sanggang Tabig
6. Saksak sa Kaliwa	Lagusan
7. Haklis	Tagang Pasumala
8. Bunot Kaluban	Sanggang Payong
9. Haklis	Tagang Pasumala
10. Hulipas	Sanggang Payong
11. Bulusok ng Dalawang Kamay	Salikop
	Aldabis sa Itaas
12. Haklis	Tagang Pasumala

Strikes and Blocks 8
(Blg. 8 - Taga at Sangga sa Abakada ng Labindalawang Taga)

A (1): Execute a downward vertical strike (Buhat Araw) with the sword, right foot forward. Keep the dagger in the high left rear position.

D (1a): Sidestep forward to the left and execute a double parry (concierto) against the sword in a left to right motion.

D (1b): Deliver a Lagusan thrust with the sword, the dagger keeping control over the opponent's sword.

A (2): Deliver an inside upward diagonal strike (Aldabis sa Ilalim) .

D (2): Execute a Salibas dagger over sword technique resulting in an intercept and check of the opponent's Aldabis sa Ilalim strike.

Strikes and Blocks 8

(Blg. 8 - Taga at Sangga sa Abakada ng Labindalawang Taga)

A (2.1): Execute a thrust with the dagger (Saksak ng Kaliwa).
Options: The sword can either be withdrawn as follows:
- under the dagger arm in preparation, the next strike will be an Aldabis sa Itaas
- back to the rear, the next strike being a Bagsak Salungat
In either case, the strike will commence from the inside upper quadrant.

D (2.1): Execute a Palis-Kaluban against the dagger thrust. Palis-Kaluban consists of the first 2 steps of the Bulalakaw technique.

D (2.1a): Vertical parry with the sword. Note the inside chambered position of the defender's dagger.

D (2.1b): Replace the sword that deflected and controlled the attacker's weapon with the dagger. The defender's sword is withdrawn and chambered below the dagger arm.

A (3): Pull back the dagger to the left rear position and execute an inside downward diagonal strike (Aldabis sa Itaas/Bagsak Salungat).

D (3): Execute a Salibas sword over dagger resulting in a Sanggang Payong with dagger check against the opponent's Aldabis sa Itaas.

Strikes and Blocks 8
(Blg. 8 - Taga at Sangga sa Abakada ng Labindalawang Taga)

A (3.1): Step forward with the left foot and deliver a thrust with the dagger (Saksak ng Kaliwa). Withdraw the sword to the upper right.

D (3.1): Intercept and counter the Saksak ng Kaliwa thrust with the tri-step Bulalakaw technique.

D (3.1a): Vertical parry with the sword. Note the inside chambered position of the defender's dagger.

D (3.1b): Replace the sword that deflected and controlled the attacker's weapon with the dagger. The defender's sword is withdrawn and chambered below the dagger arm.

D (3.1c): Keeping control of the attacker's weapon with the dagger, whip out the chambered sword to deliver a strike at the attacker's chest.

Steps D (3.1a) thru to D (3.1c) are the elements of the Bulalakaw technique.

Strikes and Blocks 8

(Blg. 8 - Taga at Sangga sa Abakada ng Labindalawang Taga)

A (4): Execute an outside upward diagonal strike (Saboy). Withdraw the dagger to the upper left side.

D (4): Execute low right to left Kambal Bagsak (Concierto - double parry) against the opponent's Saboy strike.

A (4.1) : Execute a thrust with the dagger (Saksak ng Kaliwa).

D (4.1): Execute a Palis-Kaluban against the dagger thrust. Palis-Kaluban consists of the first 2 steps of the Bulalakaw technique.

D (4.1a): Vertical parry with the sword. Note the inside chambered position of the defender's dagger.

D (4.1b): Replace the sword that deflected and controlled the attacker's weapon with the dagger. The defender's sword is withdrawn and chambered below the dagger arm.

Steps D (4.1a) thru to D (4.1c) are the elements of the Palis-Kaluban technique.

Strikes and Blocks 8

(Blg. 8 - Taga at Sangga sa Abakada ng Labindalawang Taga)

A (5): Execute an outside downward diagonal strike (Tagang San Miguel) withdrawing the dagger to the left rear position.

D (5): Step forward with the left foot and execute a Sanggang Tabig against the opponent's Tagang San Miguel.

A (6): Deliver an inside thrust with the sword (Saksak sa Kaliwa).

D (6): Execute a Lagusan sword and dagger combination against the opponent's inside sword thrust.

A (7): Execute an outside downward diagonal strike (Haklis) leaning and bringing body weight over the rear foot.

D (7): Execute a right to left Tagang Pasumala against the opponent's Haklis.

Strikes and Blocks 8
(Blg. 8 - Taga at Sangga sa Abakada ng Labindalawang Taga)

A (8): Execute an inside upward strike to the face (Bunot Kaluban) leaning forward over the front foot.

D (8): Perform a Salibas sword over dagger (Sanggang Payong) against the opponent's Bunot Kaluban strike.

A (8.1): Execute a thrust with the dagger (Saksak ng Kaliwa) keeping the sword at the right.

D (8.1): Parry the dagger thrust of the opponent with the dagger in Sikwat motion.

A (9): Execute an outside downward diagonal strike (Haklis) leaning and bringing body weight over the rear foot.

D (9): Perform a right to left Tagang Pasumala against the opponent's Haklis.

125

Strikes and Blocks 8
(Blg. 8 - Taga at Sangga sa Abakada ng Labindalawang Taga)

A (10): Execute an inside downward diagonal strike (Hulipas) while stepping forward with the left foot.

D (10): Step back with the left foot and execute a Salibas sword over dagger resulting in a Sanggang Payong with a secondary check in place against the opponent's Hulipas strike.

A (1): Execute a double descending thrust (Bulusok ng Dalawang Kamay).

D (11): Intercept the twin thrust with a high Salikop parry pushing the weapons to the left.

From the Salikop block, deliver an Aldabis sa Itaas at the opponent's head.

Strikes and Blocks 8

(Blg. 8 - Taga at Sangga sa Abakada ng Labindalawang Taga)

A (12): Step back with the left foot and execute a Haklis strike.

D(12): Step forward with the left foot and deflect/parry the Haklis with a Tagang Pasumala in a left to right motion.

127

Classic **ARNIS**

Strikes and Blocks 9

(Blg. 9 - Taga at Sangga sa Abakada ng Siyam na Taga)

Juan Aclan and Luis Cruz

9. **Taga at Sangga ng Abakada ng Siyam na Taga**
(Strikes and Blocks - Nine Step Set – Drill 9)

Attacker	*Defender*	
1. Buhat Araw	Kambal-Tabig	
	Tagang San Miguel	
2. Aldabis sa Ilalim	Salibas	
(1) Saksak ng Kaliwa		Palis-Kaluban
3. Aldabis sa Itaas/Bagsak Salungat		
	Salibas	
(2) Saksak ng Kaliwa		Bulalakaw
4. Saboy	Salikop	
	Aldabis sa Itaas	
(3) Saksak ng Kaliwa		Bulalakaw
5. Tagang San Miguel	Cadena Real	
6. Saksak sa Kaliwa	Lagusan	
7. Hulipas	Aldabis sa Itaas	
8. Bulusok ng Kalawaang Kamay	Tiklop-Pana	
	Aldabis sa Itaas	
9. Saboy	Sanggang Papalis	
	Tagang San Miguel	

Strikes and Blocks 9
(Blg. 9 - Taga at Sangga sa Abakada ng Siyam na Taga)

A (1): Execute a downward vertical strike (Buhat Araw) with the sword, right foot forward.

D (1a): Sidestep forward with the left foot and execute a double parry (Kambal Bagsak) in a left to right motion against the Buhat Araw strike.

D(1b): Once the strike has been neutralized, deliver a Tagang San Miguel (outside downward diagonal strike). The dagger ends in the high left rear position.

A (2): Deliver an inside upward diagonal strike (Aldabis sa Ilalim) .

D (2): Intercept the Aldabis sa Ilalim with a left to right Salibas dagger over sword technique.

Strikes and Blocks 9
(Blg. 9 - Taga at Sangga sa Abakada ng Siyam na Taga)

A (2.1): Execute a thrust with the dagger (Saksak ng Kaliwa).

Options: The sword can either be withdrawn as follows:

    - under the dagger arm in preparation, the next strike will be an Aldabis sa Itaas.

    - back to the rear, the next strike being a Bagsak Salungat.

In either case, the strike will commence from the inside upper quadrant.

    D (2.1) : Execute a Palis-Kaluban against the Saksak ng Kaliwa.

A (3): Pull back the dagger to the left rear position and execute an inside downward diagonal strike (Aldabis sa Itaas/Bagsak Salungat) with the sword.

    D (3): Perform a sword over dagger Salibas technique against the inside strike.

A (3.1): Step forward with the left foot and deliver a thrust with the dagger (Saksak ng Kaliwa). Withdraw the sword to the upper right

    D (3.1): Step back with the left and perform the tri-step Bulalakaw technique against the dagger thrust.

    D (3.1a): Vertical parry with the sword. Note the inside chambered position of the defender's dagger.

131

Strikes and Blocks 9
(Blg. 9 - Taga at Sangga sa Abakada ng Siyam na Taga)

D (3.1b): Replace the sword that deflected and controlled the attacker's weapon with the dagger. The defender's sword is withdrawn and chambered below the dagger arm.

D (3.1c): Keeping control of the attacker's weapon with the dagger, whip out the chambered sword to deliver a strike at the attacker's body.

Steps D (3.1a) thru to D (3.1c) are the elements of the Bulalakaw technique.

A (4): Execute an outside upward diagonal strike (Saboy). Withdraw the dagger to the upper left side.

D (4a): Block the strike with a Sanggang Salikop (augmented block).

Strikes and Blocks 9
(Blg. 9 - Taga at Sangga sa Abakada ng Siyam na Taga)

Strikes and Blocks 9
(Blg. 9 - Taga at Sangga sa Abakada ng Siyam na Taga)

D (4.1c): Keeping control of the attacker's weapon with the dagger, whip out the chambered sword to deliver a strike at the attacker's chest.

Steps D (4.1a) thru to D (4.1c) are the elements of the Bulalakaw technique.

A (5): Deliver an outside downward diagonal strike (Tagang San Miguel) .

D (5): Parry the Tagang San Miguel with the sword.

Step forward with the left foot and push the sword in an encircling motion over and around the opponent's sword and execute an inside strike (Cadena Real).

Strikes and Blocks 9

(Blg. 9 - Taga at Sangga sa Abakada ng Siyam na Taga)

A (6): Deliver an inside thrust with the sword (Saksak sa Kaliwa).

D (6): Parry the thrust with the dagger and execute a counter thrust using the Lagusan technique.

A (7): Execute an inside downward diagonal strike (Hulipas).

D(7): Step back with the left foot and execute an outside parry with the Salibas technique (sword over dagger).

A (8): Execute a double descending thrust (Bulusok ng Dalawang Kamay).

D (8a): Intercept the twin thrust with a high Salikop parry pushing the weapons to the left.

D (8b): Execute an Aldabis sa Itaas (inside downward diagonal strike).

Steps D (8a) thru D (8b) are the elements of the Tiklop-Pana technique.

A (9): Execute a low upward diagonal strike (Saboy), stepping back with the left foot.

D (9): Follow the strike with an inside low sweeping (Papalis) parry, withdrawing the right foot to avoid the opponent's strike.

Step forward and execute an outside downward diagonal strike (Tagang San Miguel).

Strikes and Blocks 10

(Blg. 10 - Taga at Sangga sa Abakada ng Sampung Taga)

Juan Aclan and Luis Cruz

10. Taga at Sangga ng Abakada ng Sampung Taga
   (Strikes and Blocks - Ten Step Set – Drill 10)

Attacker	*Defender*
1. Tagang San Miguel	Palis
2. Aldabis sa Ilalim	Haklis
3. Saboy	Salibas
	Hulipas
4. Bulusok ng Dalawang Kamay	Palis-Aldabis
5. Haklis	Tagang Pasumala
6. Saksak sa Kaliwa	Putakti
7. Haklis	Tagang Pasumala
8. Hulipas	Salibas
9. Bulusok ng Tabak	Lagusan
10. Haklis	Tagang Pasumala
	Hulipas

Strikes and Blocks 10

(Blg. 10 - Taga at Sangga sa Abakada ng Sampung Taga)

A (1): In the left forward position, execute an outside downward diagonal strike (Tagang San Miguel).

D (1): In right forward stance, execute a right to left Palis (block) shifting the body weight over the rear leg.

A (2): Step forward with the right foot and deliver an inside upward diagonal strike (Aldabis sa Ilalim). Use the momentum of the San Miguel strike to continue into the Aldabis strike.

D (2): Step back with the right foot and deliver a Haklis (outside downward diagonal strike) to intercept the strike. In actual combat a counter strike, rather than a parry, is executed and aimed at the opponent's arm.

A (3): Take a step back with the right foot and deliver a low outside diagonal upward strike (Saboy).

D (3a): Execute a right to left parry against the Saboy, bringing the body weight over the rear leg.

Strikes and Blocks 10
(Blg. 10 - Taga at Sangga sa Abakada ng Sampung Taga)

D (3b): Continue the flow of the strike then in a Concierto sword over dagger movement, switch and control the opponent's sword with the dagger, chambering the sword over the dagger arm.

D (3c): Deliver a Hulipas strike to the head. Use the dagger to keep check of the opponent's weapon.

Steps D (3a) thru D (3c) are the equivalent of a Palis-Aldabis technique commencing from a low initial parry..

A (4): Deliver a double descending thrust (Bulusok ng Dalawang Kamay),

D (4): Parry the double descending thrust (Bulusok ng Dalawang Kamay) using the tri-step Palis-Aldabis variation.

D (4.1a): Vertical parry with the sword.

Strikes and Blocks 10
(Blg. 10 - Taga at Sangga sa Abakada ng Sampung Taga)

D (4.1b): Replace the sword that deflected and controlled the attacker's weapon with the dagger. The defender's sword is withdrawn and chambered above the dagger arm.

D (4.1c): Keeping control of the attacker's weapon with the dagger, whip out the chambered sword to deliver a strike at the attacker's chest.

Steps D (4.1a) thru to D (4.1c) are the elements of the Palis-Aldabis technique.

A (5): Step back with the left foot and execute an outside downward diagonal strike (Haklis).

D (5): Execute a right to left Tagang Pasumala.

Strikes and Blocks 10
(Blg. 10 - Taga at Sangga sa Abakada ng Sampung Taga)

A (6): Execute an inside thrust with the sword (Saksak sa Kaliwa) leaning forward over the right foot.

D (6): Execute the 2nd step of the Putakti technique (Palis, Nakaw-Abaniko) to parry and counter against the inside sword thrust.

A (7): Loop and swing the sword into an outside downward diagonal strike (Haklis) bringing the body weight over the rear leg.

D (7): Block the strike with a left to right Tagang Pasumala.

A (8): Execute an inside downward diagonal strike (Hulipas) leaning forward without stepping.

D (8): Intercept the Hulipas strike with a Salibas sword over dagger technique.

Strikes and Blocks 10
(Blg. 10 - Taga at Sangga sa Abakada ng Sampung Taga)

A (9): Shift forward and deliver a descending thrust with the sword (Bulusok ng Isang Kamay).

D (9): Side-step and defend against the single descending sword thrust with the Makata technique (The Poet).

A (10): Execute an outside downward diagonal strike (Haklis).

D (10): Execute a Tagang Pasumala to intercept the Haklis strike.

Step forward and execute an Inside downward diagonal strike (Hulipas).

DIMASUPIL
(Unconquerable)

The epic form of Dimasupil is the story of the Philippine natives, nobles, freemen, warriors and slaves, fighting against the invaders from afar. The epic begins with the sighting of the invaders and the initial engagement in battle.

As the battle moves toward the main village and the chieftain's lair, the sentries remain stalwart and prevent the entry of the invaders. The warriors, with their bows, arrows, shields, spears, swords, and daggers take the bloody battle to the enemy, ensuring the safety of the tribe. The slaves, some still in chains, join in the fray and help fight against the foreign oppressors.

In the midst of this battle, nobles, freemen, warriors, and slaves, fight side by side against the invaders. Social disparity is cast aside and the blood flows and mingles freely. In the end, the slaves, fighting heroically to defend their masters and their clan, prove themselves loyal and able warriors and are rewarded their freedom.

This form and the corresponding individual drills and techniques have been added to this publication as supplementary materials to Placido Yambao's original manuscript. Many of the techniques that have for so long remained "hidden" in Yambao's legacy was the result of Yambao's assumption that the reader/practitioner is already well-versed in and familiar with Yambao's mother art, the art of "Adwang Mutun" or Sinawali.

DIMASUPIL
(Unconquerable)

Harap Hilaga
Facing North

Simula - Start
Harap Hilaga - Facing North

1-2 Bulalakaw
The Comet

3-5 Putakti
The Hornet

DIMASUPIL
(Unconquerable)

6 Lagusan
Tunnel Thrust

7-9 Salikop-Pana
Augmented Block, The Archer

10-12 Bulalakaw Sinawali
The Comet, Staggered/Woven Strikes

13-15 Putakti
The Hornet

145

DIMASUPIL
(Unconquerable)

Harap Hilaga
Facing North

16 Lagusan
Tunnel Thrust

17-19 Salikop-Pana
Augmented Block, The Archer

20-22 Bulalakaw Sinawali
The Comet, Staggered/Woven Strikes

Tanaw Kanluran
Eyes West

Tanaw Silangan
Eyes East

23-24 Ang Tanod
The Sentry

DIMASUPIL
(Unconquerable)

Harap Kanluran
Facing West

25 Ang Mamamana
The Archer

26 Kalasag at Sibat
Shield and Spear

27-28 Kalasag/Pluma, Bagsak
Shield and Drop Strike

29-30 Palis-Tusok
Parry and Thrust

31 Sima't Tulay
Scythe Parry and
Thrust

32 Ang Makata
The Poet

33 Fraile-Sungkite
Friar's Blessing and
Thrust

34 Nakaw-Tusok
Inside Parry and
Thrust

DIMASUPIL

Harap Silangan
Facing East

(Unconquerable)

35 Ang Mamamana
The Archer

36 Kalasag at Sibat
Shield and Spear

37-38 Kalasag/Pluma, Bagsak
Shield and Drop Strike

39-40 Palis-Tusok
Parry and Thrust

41 Sima't Tulay
Scythe Parry and
Thrust

42 Ang Makata
The Poet

43 Fraile-Sungkite
Friar's Blessing and
Thrust

44 Nakaw-Tusok
Inside Parry and
Thrust

DIMASUPIL
(Unconquerable)

45-47 Ang Mandirigmang Alipin
The Warrior Slave

Harap Kanluran
Facing West

Harap Timog
Facing South

48 Ang Maharlika
The Nobleman

49 Ang Mandirigma
The Warrior

Harap Timog
Facing South

Mula sa Harap
From the Front

49 Ang Mandirigma
The Warrior

DIMASUPIL
(Unconquerable)

Harap Timog
Facing South

50-51 Tusok Alakdan
Scorpion's Thrust and Sting

52-53 Salikop-Makata
Augmented Block and Poet's Thrust

54 Lagusan
Tunnel Thrust

55-56 Salikop, Sumbrada-Sungkite
Augmented Block, Roof Block and Thrust

57 Nakaw-Bagsak
Inside Parry and Strike

Pihit Kanan, Harap Hilaga
Turn Right, Face North

58 Nakaw-Bagsak
Inside Parry and Strike

59 Ang Mandirigma
The Warrior

DIMASUPIL
(Unconquerable)

Harap Hilaga
Facing North

60-61 Tusok Alakdan
Scorpion's Thrust and Sting

62-63 Salikop-Makata
Augmented Block and Poet's Thrust

64 Lagusan
Tunnel Thrust

65-66 Salikop, Sumbrada-Sungkite
Augmented Block, Roof Block and Thrust

67-69 Ang Mandirigmang Alipin
The Warrior Slave

DIMASUPIL
(Unconquerable)

Harap Hilaga
Facing North

(70-71 De Cuerdas)
Rebounding Strikes

(72-74 Redonda)
Whirlwind Strikes

(75 - 76 Bukang Liwayway)
Sunrise Strikes

70 - 76 Tanikalang Itim
The Black Chain

DIMASUPIL
(Unconquerable)

Harap Hilaga
Facing North

(77 - 78 De Cuerdas)
Rebounding Strikes

(79 - 81 Redonda)
Whirlwind Strikes

(82 - 83 Bukang Liwayway)
Sunrise Strikes

77 - 83 Tanikalang Itim
The Black Chain

DIMASUPIL
(Unconquerable)

Harap Hilaga
Facing North

84 Katapusan
End

Featured SINAWALI Techniques

The following section is a detailed presentation of the Sinawali-based techniques used in Placido Yambao's Strikes and Blocks (Taga at Sangga). Most of these techniques are preserved in the advanced Sinawali form known as "Dimasupil".

Bulalakaw
(The Comet/Meteor)

Putakti
(The Hornet)

Lagusan
(Tunnel Thrust)

Redonda Salok-Saboy
(Reversed Whirlwind Strikes)

Salikop-Pana
(Augmented Block with The Archer)

Ang Tanod
(The Sentry)

Kalasag/Palis-Tusok
(Shield/Parry and Thrust)

Pluma-/Bagsak
(Pen/Wing/Outside Roof Block and Drop Strike)

Sima-Tulay, Makata
(Hooking/Scythe Parry and Thrust, The Poet)

Fraile, Nakaw-Tusok
(The Friar's Blessing, Inside/Covert Thrust))

Salikop, Makata
(Augmented Block, The Poet)

Salikop, Sumbrada-Sungkite
(Augmented Block, Roof Block and Thrust)

Salibas - Salisok
(Inward/Outward Circles)

Bulalakaw
(The Comet/Meteor)

Step forward, off-center and execute a parry with the lead weapon. Chamber the secondary weapon inside and behind the lead weapon.

Switch and check with the secondary weapon, and chamber the lead weapon under the secondary.

Execute an overhead parry with the secondary weapon and deliver a mid/low strike with the lead weapon.

Putakti
(The Hornet)

Step forward, off-center and execute a high inside parry with the lead weapon and a middle thrust with the secondary weapon.

Withdraw and loop the secondary weapon into an inside high strike while keeping check and control with the lead weapon.

Switch lead position and execute a reverse low parry and simultaneously deliver an outside high strike.

Lagusan
(Tunnel Thrust)

Step forward, off-center and execute a parry with the lead weapon. Execute a thrust with the secondary weapon inside and behind the lead parry.

Execute a strike with lead weapon and withdraw the secondary weapon in a circular overhead (vertex) motion.

Continue the looping overhead motion into an outside striking motion while simultaneously switching forward position.

Redonda Salok-Saboy
(Reversed Whirlwind Strikes)

Execute an inside parry with the secondary weapon while delivering an outside mid-level upward diagonal strike with the lead weapon.

Execute a mid-level upward diagonal strike with the secondary weapon and chamber the lead weapon under the secondary.

Withdraw the secondary weapon and deliver a mid-level inside upward diagonal strike with the lead weapon.

Salikop-Pana
(Augmented Block with The Archer)

Step forward, off-center and execute an inside augmented block with the secondary weapon executing a low block, reinforced by the lead weapon.

Reverse the lead weapon into a high inside reverse parry followed by the secondary weapon in a high outside vertical parry position.

Execute an inside downward strike with the lead weapon while transferring control to the secondary weapon.

Ang Tanod
(The Sentry)

Execute a high outside parry.

Execute an inside high parry and withdraw the outside parry behind the inside high parry.

Repeat the high outside parry and chamber the inside parry under the arm executing the outside parry.

Continue the outward movement into an outside horizontal strike with the right arm chambered underneath in a vertical position.

Kalasag/Palis-Tusok
(Shield/Parry and Thrust)

Execute a high inside parry with the lead weapon. Chamber or position the secondary weapon inside and behind the lead weapon.

Transfer control to the secondary weapon and execute a mid-level horizontal outward slashing movement with the lead weapon.

Keep control with the secondary weapon and continue with the slashing motion of the lead weapon keeping its tip pointed towards the opponent.

Convert the slashing motion into an inward high thrust.

Pluma-/Bagsak
(Pen/Wing/Outside Roof Block and Drop Strike)

Step off-center forward and intercept the incoming strike with an inside parry using the lead weapon. Position secondary weapon for reprisal as well as auxilliary defense.

Keeping check with the lead weapon, deliver a downward strike with the secondary weapon.

Withdraw the secondary weapon in a vertex (sinalakot) movement and deliver an inside downward strike with the original lead weapon.

Step forward or shift position and deliver an outside downward strike with the new lead weapon.

Sima-Tulay, Makata
(Hooking/Scythe Parry and Thrust, The Poet)

Step forward, off-center and intercept the incoming strike with an inside scythe parry (sima). Position secondary weapon for a counter-thrust.

Continue the deflection of the opponent's attack and deliver a thrust to the body from the reverse stance.

Convert the thrust to an outside scythe parry (sima) and deliver an inside thrust (makata) with the lead weapon.

Fraile, Nakaw-Tusok

(The Friar's Blessing, Inside/Covert Thrust))

Execute a high inside parry with the lead weapon while stepping diagonally forward.	Loop the parry into an upward rising cut (fraile) to draw the opponent's attention and deliver a lunge thrust with the new lead weapon.	Step forward or switch forward position and drop the raised weapon into a strike or inside parry and deliver a thrust from behind the lead weapon.	Withdraw the thrust into an overhead block and deliver a low strike with the lead weapon ending in Mandirigma (warrior) stance/position.

Salikop, Makata
(Augmented Block, The Poet)

Sidestep and execute a low augmented block, reinforcing the outside weapon with the lead, inside weapon.

Convert the lead weapon into a lunge thrust while maintaining guard/defense with the secondary weapon.

Salikop, Sumbrada-Sungkite
(Augmented Block, Roof Block and Thrust)

Side-step and execute a low augmented block reinforcing the outside weapon with the lead, inside weapon.

Execute a high roof block with the lead weapon and deliver a thrust with the secondary weapon.

Drop the raised weapon into a strike or an inside parry and execute a thrust behind the lead weapon.

Salibas - Salisok
(Inward/Outward Circles)

Diagonally side-step forward and execute a high inside parry with the lead weapon while delivering a simultaneous counter strike with the secondary weapon.

Continue the downward motion into a low inside quadrant block.

Side step to the right and execute a lead weapon parry while delivering a secondary weapon counter strike.

Step back and execute a low outside quadrant parry with the lead weapon.

Deliver a counter strike at the opponent's weapon arm with the secondary weapon.

Continue the upward motion into a high inside quadrant block.

Side step to the right and execute a lead weapon parry while delivering a secondary weapon counter strike.

Resume ready position.

Glossary

Abakada	Alphabet; the abc's; basic drills
Abaniko	Fan; fan strike; fanning motion
Adwang Mutun	Two sticks; another name for Sinawali
Alakdan	Scorpion; an overhead whipping strike
Aldabis sa Ilalim	Inside upward diagonal strike
Aldabis sa Itaas	Inside downward diagonal strike
Alipin	Slave
Alpabeto	Alphabet; names of strikes
Ang	The (article)
Anyo	Form; shape
Baguhan	Beginner; novice; a basic Sinawali technique
Bagsak	Drop strike
Bagsak Salungat	Ellipse drop strike
Balangkas	Foundation drills
Balaraw	Dagger
Bartikal	Backhand/whip strike
Bughaw	Blue
Buhat Araw	Overhead strike
Bukang Liwayway	Sunrise strikes; high and low strikes
Bulalakaw	Comet; meteor; a high to mid-level parry, switch and strike combination
Bulalakaw-Pana	A sword over dagger variation of Bulalakaw see Palis-Aldabis
Bulalakaw-Sinawali	Bulalakaw performed with three distinct stages
Bulusok ng Dalawang Kamay	Double/twin descending/avalanche thrusts
Bulusok ng Isang Kamay	Single descending/avalanche thrust
Bunot Kaluban	Drawing of the sword
Cadena Real	A two-step parry and strike technique
Daga	Dagger
De Cuerdas	Rebounding strike combinations
Defensa ofensiva	see Sangga at Patama
Enganyo	A feint; a trap
Fraile	Friar; an upward vertical cut
Fraile-Sungkite	A combination upward cut and thrust
Fraile-Tusok	see Fraile-Sungkite
Ginto	Gold
Haklis	Scooping downward strike
Hilaga	North
Hulipas	Inside downward diagonal strike
Ibaba	Below; low
Itaas	Above; high
Itim	Black
Kalasag	Shield
Kaliwa	Left
Kanan	Right
Kanluran	West
Kambal	Twin; double
Kambal Bagsak	Double/twin drop strike
Kambal Tabig	Double/twin push/deflection

Glossary

Katapusan	End; finish
Labanang Malapitan	Close quarters combat
Labanang Malayuan	Long range combat
Lagusan	Tunnel thrust; thrust over parry
Lakantalaturo	Chief instructor
Langit at Lupa	A three step high and low strike combination; Used to indicate any high and low combination
Larga Mano	Long range fighting
Magbabayo	One who wields a pestle; downward figure 8 strikes
Maharlika	Noble; nobility
Makata	The poet; inside thrust
Mamamana	The archer
Mandirigma	Warrior
Mata	Eye
Muestracion	Demonstration of individual skills through striking and blocking
Nakaw-Tusok	A variation of Lagusan; inside thrust
Palis	To sweep; deflect
Palis-Aldabis	A sword over dagger parry, check and counter
Palis-Kaluban	A sword under dagger parry and check
Palis ng Dalawang Kamay	A double sweeping/deflecting parry
Palis ng Tabak	A parry/deflection with the sword
Palis-Tungkod	A two-step sweeping deflecting parry (the sword is extended forward under the left arm)
Palis-Tusok	A parry and thrust combination
Pana	Arrow; bow and arrow
Pasumala	A near miss; deflection
Payong	Umbrella; roof block
Pluma	Pen; outside wing block
Pula	Red
Punong guro	Chief/head instructor
Putakti	The Hornet; a triple combination parry and strike technique
Puti	White
Redonda	Whirlwind Strikes
Redonda Salok-Saboy	Reverse whirlwind strikes
Regla	Form
Rompido	Close quarters combat
Sablay	Low outside scooping/horizontal strike
Saboy	Mid-level outside upward diagonal strike
Salok-Saboy	Draw and throw; reverse figure eight strikes
Saksak	Thrust
Saksak ng Kaliwa	Thrust with the left weapon (dagger)
Saksak sa gawing Kaliwa	Inside thrust (sword)
Saksak sa gawing Kanan	Outside thrust (sword)
Salibas	Outward circles; a contraction of salising palabas
Salikop	Augmented block
Salikop-Makata	Augmented block with inside thrust
Salikop-Pana	Low augmented block with high augmented block and strike
Salikop-Saliwa	A reversed position augmented block

Glossary

Salisi	In opposite directions
Salising Palabas	see Salibas
Salising Papasok	see Salisok
Salisok	Inward circles; a contraction of salising papasok
Sangga	Block or parry
Sanggang Papalis	see Palis
Sanggang Payong	see Payong
San Miguel	Outside diagonal strike
Sangga at Patama	Demonstration of striking, blocking and corresponding counter-attack
Sanggang Taga	A strike used as a parry/block
Sayaw	Form; dance
Sibat	Spear
Sikwat	A reverse parry
Sikwat-Abaniko	A reverse parry with simultaneous fan strike
Sikwat-Aldabis	A low reverse parry variation of Palis-Aldabis
Sikwat-Bagsak	A reverse parry with simultaneous drop strike
Silangan	East
Sima	Hooking/Scythe parry or thrust
Sima-Tulay	Combination sima and tulay parry and thrust
Sima't Tulay	see Sima-Tulay
Simula	Start; beginning
Sinalakot	In a vertex/conical fashion
Sinauali	Spelling variation of Sinawali
Sinawali	Woven; double weapon fighting art; see Adwang Mutun
Sulong	Forward; step forward
Sumbrada	Roof block
Sumbrada-Sungkite	A roof block and thrust combination
Sungkite	Thrust; generic term for thrust techniques
Tabak	Native sword
Tabas-Talahib	Outside horizontal strike
Tagang Alanganin	Inside horizontal strike
Tagang Buhat Araw	see Buhat Araw
Tagang Pahulipas	see Hulipas
Tagang Papalis	A sweeping/deflecting strike
Tagang Pasumala	see Pasumala
Tabig	Push; deflect
Tabig ng kaliwa	A controlling push/check with the dagger
Tagang San Miguel	see San Miguel
Tanaw	Visible; look towards
Tanikala	Chain; a series of techniques
Tanod	The sentry; a tri-step parry and strike technique
Tatang	Elder; a respectful title/prefix for elders or seniors
Tigpas	Low inside horizontal strike
Tiklop-Pana	High reverse augmented parry and counter
Timog	South
Tulay	Bridge thrust; thrust underneath parry
Tusok-Alakdan	A middle thrust and overhead strike combination
Tusok-Fraile	A thrust combined with a Fraile enganyo
Urong	Retreat; step back